Foundry Work; A Practical Handbook On Standard Foundry Practice, Including Hand And Machine Molding; Cast Iron, Malleable Iron, Steel And Brass Castings; Foundry Management; Etc.

Stimpson, William C, Gray, Burton L. (Burton Linwood)

Nabu Public Domain Reprints:

You are holding a reproduction of an original work published before 1923 that is in the public domain in the United States of America, and possibly other countries. You may freely copy and distribute this work as no entity (individual or corporate) has a copyright on the body of the work. This book may contain prior copyright references, and library stamps (as most of these works were scanned from library copies). These have been scanned and retained as part of the historical artifact.

This book may have occasional imperfections such as missing or blurred pages, poor pictures, errant marks, etc. that were either part of the original artifact, or were introduced by the scanning process. We believe this work is culturally important, and despite the imperfections, have elected to bring it back into print as part of our continuing commitment to the preservation of printed works worldwide. We appreciate your understanding of the imperfections in the preservation process, and hope you enjoy this valuable book.

FIXED CROSS-RAIL MILLING MACHINE MILLING AUTOMOBILE CASTINGS

FOUNDRY WORK

A Practical Handbook on Standard Foundry Practice,
Including Hand and Machine Molding; Cast
Iron, Malleable Iron, Steel, and Brass
Castings; Foundry Manage-
ment; Etc.

REVISED BY

BURTON L. GRAY

INSTRUCTOR IN FOUNDRY PRACTICE, WORCESTER POLYTECHNIC INSTITUTE
MEMBER, FOUNDRYMEN'S ASSOCIATION

ILLUSTRATED

AMERICAN TECHNICAL SOCIETY
CHICAGO
1918

COPYRIGHT, 1916, 1918, BY
AMERICAN TECHNICAL SOCIETY

COPYRIGHTED IN GREAT BRITAIN
ALL RIGHTS RESERVED

JUN 26 1918

©Cl.A497907

INTRODUCTION

THE making of a metal casting seems like a very simple operation—given a pattern, a flask, a supply of molding sand, and some molten metal, presto! it is done—but a little study develops the fact that there are few industries where more depends upon shop kinks and the many other essential things which make up a broad knowledge of a distinct trade than in foundry work. The industry, as such, is as old as our knowledge of brass and iron, the former having been made into castings from earliest times. Casting methods, however, have partaken of the general mechanical development of the last few years and today there is no comparison as to the quality of castings, the complexity of the patterns cast, and the speed of manufacture, with the work of a few years ago.

¶ In this article the methods of hand molding have been carefully discussed, including the many questions of pattern construction which are more or less closely associated with foundry work. The presentation also includes the uses of the various types of molding machines, which have become so popular within the last few years. Malleable iron practice has now become well standardized and this type of casting, particularly for small work requiring much duplication, is very important. An excellent discussion of steel castings is particularly pertinent as this type of casting is fast displacing drop forgings for many classes of work.

¶ Altogether the article represents a well-rounded and thoroughly up-to-date discussion of this important subject. The original author and the reviser, both men of broad experience, have combined to give the reader the benefit of their knowledge and it is the hope of the publishers that the book will be found instructive and interesting to the practical foundry man as well as to the general reader.

CONTENTS

	PAGE
Molding practice	1
Main branches	1
Molding equipment	3
Classes	3
Molding sand	5, 6
Core sand	6
Graphite	7
Charcoal	7
Sea coal	7
Distinction	7
Fire clay	7
Parting dusts	8
Core binders	9
Tools	9
Flasks	9
Shovel	12
Rammers	13
Finishing tools	14
Clamps	17
Molding processes	18
Sand mixture	18
Sifting	19
Ramming	20
Gating	24
Shrinkage heads	26
Pressure in molds	27
Common defects in castings	31
Typical molding problems	31
Flat joint	32
Coping out	35
Sand match	36
Split-pattern molds	38
Floor bedding	42
Open mold	45

CONTENTS

	PAGE
Core work	46
Materials	46
Equipment	48
Conditions of use	50
Methods of making	53
Cylindrical cores	58
Setting chaplets	60
Projecting cores	60
Hanging cores	61
Bottom-anchored cores	61
Duplicating castings	66
Practical requisites in hand molding	66
Use of molding machines	67
Dry-sand work	89
Characteristic features	89
Molding engine cylinder	89
Making barrel core	92
Loam molding	94
Rigging	94
Materials	97
Principles of work	99
Simple mold	102
Intricate mold	104
Casting operations	109
Furnace parts	109
Blast	112
Running a heat	116
Foundry ladles	118
Pouring	119
Chemical analysis	123
Calculation of mixture	124
Fuel	126
Sand mixing	127
Cleaning castings	131
Steel work	136
Present development	136
Processes	136
Characteristics of metal	136

CONTENTS

	PAGE
Steel molds	137
Facing mixtures	137
Packing	139
Cores	141
Steel castings	141
Running a heat	141
Setting up molds	143
Cleaning castings	144
Annealing	144
Malleable practice	145
Comparative characteristics of metal	145
Testing	146
Production processes	148
Molding methods	149
Methods of melting	152
Iron mixture	156
Variation from gray-iron practice	159
Cleaning castings	160
Annealing	161
Finishing	167
Brass work	167
Metals	168
Mixtures	170
Production	171
Molding materials	171
Equipment	172
Examples of work	175
Melting	176
Cleaning	181
Shop management	182
Governing factors	182
Molding divisions	184
Materials	186
Handling systems	186
Cleaning department	187
Performance	188
Accident prevention	189
Checking	190
Keep's mechanical analysis	190
Arbitration-bar tests	191

FOUNDRY WORK

PART I

MOLDING PRACTICE

Introductory. *Foundry work* is the name applied to that branch of engineering which deals with melting metal and pouring it in liquid form into sand molds to shape it into castings of all descriptions.

In the manufacture of modern machinery three classes of castings are employed, each one having its individual physical properties, such as strength, toughness, durability, etc. These castings are as follows: gray iron; copper alloys, i.e., brass, bronze, etc.; and mild steel. By far the greatest number of castings made are of gray iron, that is, iron which may be machined directly as it comes from the mold without any further heat treatment.

The main purpose of this book is to explain the underlying principles involved in making molds for gray-iron castings, and the mixing and melting of the metals for such castings. The articles on Malleable Cast Iron as well as the articles on Brass Founding and Steel Casting emphasize only those features of the methods used which differ from gray-iron foundry practice. The article on Shop Management is intended to set students thinking on this subject; because the whole trend of modern shop practice is toward specialization and system in handling every department of the work, in order to increase efficiency and reduce cost.

DIVISIONS OF IRON MOLDING

Main Branches. There are four main branches in gray iron molding: (1) green-sand work; (2) core work; (3) dry-sand molding; and (4) loam work.

Green-Sand Molding. The cheapest quickest method of forming the general run of castings is by green-sand molding. Damp molding sand is rammed over the pattern, and suitable flasks are used for handling the mold. When the pattern is withdrawn the mold is finished, and the metal is poured while the efficiency of the mold is still retained by reason of this dampness. The mold may be poured as soon as made; and in case of necessity it may be held over a day or more depending upon its size. If the sand dries out, the mold should not be poured.

Core Making. Core making supplements molding. It deals with the construction of separate shapes in sand which form holes, cavities, or pockets, in the castings. Such shapes are called *cores*. They are held firmly in position by the sand of the mold itself or by the use of chaplets. Core sand is of a different composition from molding sand. It is shaped in wooden molds called *core boxes*. All cores are baked in an oven before they can be used. The whole detail of their construction is so different from that of a mold, that core making is a distinct trade—a trade, however, that is generally considered a stepping stone to that of molding. Boys usually begin to serve their time in the core shop

Dry-Sand Molding. Dry-sand molding is the term applied to that class of work where a flask is used, but a layer of core sand mixture is used as a facing next to the pattern and the joint, and the entire mold is baked before pouring. This drives off all moisture and gives hard clean surfaces to shape the iron. It is used where heavy work having considerable detail is to be cast, or where the rush of metal or the bulk of it might injure a mold of green sand. Dry-sand molds are usually made up one day, baked over night, and assembled and cast the next day.

Loam Work. Loam work is the term applied to molds built of bricks carried on heavy iron plates. The facing is put on the bricks in the form of mortar and shaped by sweeps or patterns depending upon the design of the piece to be cast. All parts of the mold are baked, rendering the surfaces hard and clean. After being assembled, these brick molds must be rammed up on the outside with green sand in a pit or casing to prevent their bursting out under the casting pressure. Simple molds can be made up one day, assembled, rammed up and poured the next, but it usually takes 3 or 4 days and sometimes as many weeks to turn out a casting.

Loam work is used for the heaviest class of iron castings for which, on account of the limited number wanted, or the simplicity of the shape, it would not pay to make complete patterns and use a flask. In some cases the intricacy of the design makes a pattern necessary, and size alone excludes the use of sand and flasks.

Selection of Method. No hard and fast rules exist for the selection of the method by which a piece will be molded. Especially with large work, the question whether it shall be put up in green sand, dry sand, or loam, often depends upon local shop conditions. The point to consider is: How can the best casting for the purpose be made for the least money, considering the facilities at hand to work with?

MOLDING EQUIPMENT

MATERIALS

Before taking up the making of molds, let us consider briefly the materials used, where they are obtained, and what is their particular service in the mold. Also we shall describe the principal tools used by the molder in working up these materials into molds.

Classes. There are three general classes of materials for molding kept in stock in the foundry, as tabulated herewith:

Molding Materials

Sands	Facings	Miscellaneous

Molding sands
  Light
  Medium
  Strong
Free sands
  Sharp or Fire
  Beach sand
	Graphite
	Charcoal
	Sea coal
		Fire clay
		Parting dust
		Burnt sand
		Charcoal
		Partamol
		Core binders

Sands

Quality. All sands are formed by the breaking up of rocks due to the action of natural forces, such as frost, wind, rain, and the action of water.

Fragments of rocks on the mountain sides, broken off by action of frost are washed into mountain streams by rainfall. Here they grind against each other and pieces thus chipped off are carried by the rush of the current down into the rivers. Tumbled along by the rapid current of the upper river, the sand will finally be deposited where the stream flows more gently through the low land stretches

TABLE I
Proportions of Elements in Sands

Elements	Fire Sand (per cent)	Molding Sands				Core Sand (per cent)
		Iron Work			Brass	
		Light (per cent)	Medium (per cent)	Heavy (per cent)	Light (per cent)	
(a) Silica............SiO$_2$	98.04	82.21	85.85	88.40	78.86	85.50
Alumina (clay)....Al$_2$O$_3$	1.40	9.48	8.37	6.30	7.89	2.65
Iron oxide........Fe$_2$O$_3$	.06	4.25	2.32	2.00	5.45	.85
Lime oxide........CaO	.20	....	.50	.78	.50	....
(b) Lime carbonate..CaCO$_3$	....	.68	.29	....	1.46	2.65
Magnesia.........MgO	.16	.32	.81	.50	1.18	4.27
Soda.............Na$_2$O	....	.09	.10	....	.13	.04
Potash...........K$_2$O	....	.05	.03	....	.09	.04
Combined water....H$_2$O	.14	2.64^a	1.68	1.73	3.80	2.00
Organic matter.........		.28	.15	.04	.64	1.00
Specific gravity........	2.592	2.652	2.645	2.630	2.640	
Degree of fineness......		85	66	46	95	

below the hills. Here the slight agitation tends to cause the finer sand and the clay to settle lower and lower down in the bed. Thus we find beds that have been formed in ages past; possibly with a top soil formed over them, so long have they been deposited. But on removing this top soil we find gravel or coarse sand on top; this merges into finer sand and this again finally into a bed of clay.

Rocks, however, are very complex in their composition, and sands contain most of the elements of the rocks of which they are fragments. For this reason molding sands in different parts of the United States vary considerably.

A good molding sand first of all, should be refractory, that is, capable of withstanding the heat of molten metal. It should be porous to allow the escape of gases from the mold. It should have a certain amount of clay to give it bond or strength, and should have an even grain. All of these properties will vary according to the class of work for which the sand is used.

Elements. The two important chemical elements in such sands are silica, which is the heat-resisting element, and alumina, or clay, which gives the bond. Other elements which are found in the molding sands are oxide of iron, oxide of lime, lime carbonate, soda potash, combined water, etc. The analyses shown in Table I, made by

W. G. Scott, give an idea of the proportions of these elements in the different foundry sands.

Silica alone is a fire-resisting element, but it has no bond. These other elements help in forming the bond. But under heat, silica combines and fuses with them, forming silicates. These silicates melt at a much lower temperature than does free silica. Therefore with sands carrying much limestone in their make up, or with those containing much oxide of iron, soda potash, etc , the molten iron will burn in more, making it more difficult to clean the casings.

The limestone combinations also go to pieces under heat, tending to make the sand crumble, which may result in dirty castings.

The proportions given in Table I must not be considered as absolutely fixed, for no two samples of sand, even from the same bed, will analyze exactly alike. The table is instructive, however, because it indicates the reasons why the different sands are especially adapted to the use to which they are put in practice.

Fire Sand. Such sand is used in the daubing mixture for repairing inside of cupola and ladles, and should be in the highest degree refractory, and should contain as little matter as possible that would tend to make it fuse or melt.

Light Molding Sand. This sand is used for castings such as stove plate, etc., which may have very finely carved detail on their surfaces, but are thin. The sand should be very fine to bring out this detail; it must be strong, i.e., high in clay, so that the mold will retain every detail as the metal rushes in. On the other hand, the work will cool so quickly that after the initial escape of the air and steam there will be very little gas to come off through the sand.

Medium Sand. Sand of this grade is used in bench work and light floor work, for making machinery castings having from $\frac{1}{2}$- to 2-inch sections. These will have less fine detail, so the sand may be coarser than in the previous case. The bond should still be fairly strong to preserve the shape of the mold, but the tendency of the large proportion of clay to choke the vent will be offset by the larger size of the grain. This vent must be provided for because the metal will remain hot in the mold for a longer time and will cause gases to form during the whole of its cooling period.

Heavy Sand. This grade of sand is used for the largest iron castings. Here the sand must be high in silica and the grain coarse, because the heat of the molten metal must be resisted by the sand, and gases must be carried off through the sand for a very long time after pouring. The amount of bond or clay must be small or it will cause the sand to cake and choke these gases. The detail is generally so large that the lack of bond is compensated for by the use of gaggers, nails, etc. The coarse grain is rendered smooth on the mold surface by careful slicking.

Core Sand. Core sand, often almost entirely surrounded by metal, must be quite refractory but have very little clay bond. This bond would make the sand cake, choking the vent, and render it difficult of removal from a cavity when cleaning the casting. Compared with medium molding sand, it shows higher in silica, although having less than half the proportion of alumina

Free Sands. Sands having practically no clay in them are called *free sands*. Of these there are two kinds in use: river sands, and beach sands

River Sand. The grains of river sand retain the sharp fractured appearance of chipped rock, and these little sharp grains help much in making a strong core because the sharp angular grains interlock one with another. River sand is used on the larger core work

Beach Sand Beach sand is considerably used in coast sections because it is relatively inexpensive, but its grains are all rounded smooth by the incessant action of the waves. It will pack together only as will so many minute marbles. For this reason it is used only for small cores.

Facings

Function. *Foundry facing* is the term given to materials applied to or mixed with the sand which comes in contact with the melted metal. The object is to give a smooth surface to the casting. They accomplish this in two ways: (1) by filling in the pores between the sand, thus giving a smooth surface to the mold face before the metal is poured; and (2) by burning very slowly under the heat of the metal, forming a thin film of gas between the sand and iron during the cooling process. This prevents the iron burning into the sand and causes the sand to separate from the casting when cold.

Different forms of carbon are used for this purpose because carbon will glow and give off gases, but it will not melt. The principal facings are graphite, charcoal, and sea coal.

Graphite. Graphite is a mineral form of carbon. It is mined from the earth and shipped in lumps which are blacker than coal and are soft and greasy like a lump of clay. The purest graphite comes from the Island of Ceylon, India. There are several beds, however, in the coal fields of North America.

Charcoal. Charcoal is a vegetable form of carbon. It is made by forming a shapely pile of wood, covering this over with earth and sod, with the exception of four small openings at the bottom and one at the top. The pile is set on fire and the wood smoulders for days. This burns off the gases from the wood, leaving the fibrous structure charred but not consumed. Charcoal burning is done in the lumbering districts. The charcoal for foundry facings should be made from hard wood.

Sea Coal. Although sea coal contains a high per cent of carbon, it is less pure than the other facings and gives off much more gas. Sea coal is made from the screenings from the soft-coal breakers. The coal should be carefully selected by the manufacturer and be free from slate and very low in sulphur.

Distinction. All facings are manufactured by putting the raw materials through a series of crushers, tumbling mills, or old-fashioned burr stone mills, and then screening them. The finest facings are bolted much as flour is.

In the shop the molder distinguishes between facings or blackings, and facing sand. *Blacking* consists of graphite or charcoal, and is applied to the finished surface of a mold or core. *Facing sand* is the name given to a mixture of new sand, old sand, and sea coal, which in the heavier classes of work forms the first layer of sand next the pattern.

The use of the different facings will be clearly seen from the tabulation on page 8.

Miscellaneous Materials

Fire Clay. Fire clay comes from the same source that sand does. It is almost pure oxide of alumina, which is separated out from the sand by a combination of the chemical action of the waters of the streams. Fire clay has traces of the other impurities men-

Characteristics of Facings

Material	Uses	Action
Charcoal	Good facing for light molds; dusted on from bag after pattern is drawn. Mixed with molasses water for wash for small cores and dry-sand work. Mixed with some graphite and clay wash for blacking for heavy dry-sand and loam work; slicked over with tools. May be used as a parting dust on joint of bench molds.	Burns at low enough temperature to be effective before thin work cools. Resists moisture; prevents sand surfaces from sticking together.
Graphite	Good facing for bench molds; dusted on from bag; good for medium and heavy green-sand work. Applied with camel's hair brush, and slicked over with tools. As heavy blacking for dry-sand and loam work, used as above.	Good on heavier green sand because it is more refractory than charcoal, but still forms gas enough to keep metal from burning into sand.
Sea Coal	Mixed with facing sand in proportions from 1:6 to 1:12. See section on Molding.	Helps to force vents through sand when mold is first poured, and prevents strong sand of the facing from caking, because it continues to throw off gas after casting has solidified.

tioned in the analysis of molding sands. It is found in the lowest strata of the deposit beds. It is used to mix with fire sand in the proportion of 1 to 4 as the daubing mixture for cupola and ladles.

Clay wash is a mixture of fire clay and water. The test for mixing it is to dip the finger into the wash and then withdraw it, whereupon there should be an even film of clay deposited on the finger. Clay wash is used as the basis of heavy blackings. It is used as follows: for wetting crossbars of flasks; for breaks in sand where a repair is to be made; to wet up the dry edges of ladle linings when repairing with fresh daubing mixture; in fact, any place where a strong bond is required at some particular spot.

Parting Dusts. Parting sands or parting dusts must contain no bond. They are used to throw on to the damp surfaces of molds which must separate one from another. They prevent these surfaces formed of high bond sands from sticking to each other.

The cheapest parting sand, and by far the most commonly used, is obtained by putting some burnt core sand, from the cleaning shed, through a fine sieve.

Beach sand is also used as a parting sand, but the rounded nature of its grain weakens the molding sands more than does burnt core sand.

Charcoal facing dusted from a bag makes an excellent parting dust on fine work.

A dust manufactured expressly for the purpose and called "Partainol" is the most perfect material for fine work. This is applied from a dust bag. It is not only useful for sand joints, but is a great help if there is a deep lift on a pattern where the sand is liable to stick, or for a troublesome box in the core room.

Core Binders. Although the materials for this purpose—flour, rosin, oil, etc.—are on the purchasing list of the general foundry buyer, for the purposes of this article they will be explained in detail under Core Work.

TOOLS

Under this heading only the hand tools and equipment used by the molder in putting up his mold are described. The mechanical appliances for reducing labor are described in a later section.

Flasks. To use sand economically for molds, sets of open frames called *flasks* are used. Flasks consist of two or more such boxes. The lower box is called the *drag* or *nowel*, the upper box is called the *cope*. If there are intermediate parts to the flask they are called *cheeks*. Flasks are fitted with pins and sockets so that they will always register.

Snap Flask. For small castings the molds are rammed up on benches or projecting brackets. Such work is termed *bench work* and the flasks are usually what are known as *snap flasks*. They range in size from 9 by 12 inches to 18 by 20 inches. As is seen in Fig. 1, these flasks hinge on one corner and have catches on the diagonal corner. The advantage of the snap flask is that any number of molds may be put up with but one flask, and the flask removed as each mold is completed. There are several good snap flasks to be had on the market. Many foundries, however, make up their own.

Each size of flask should have at least one smooth straight board called the *mold board*, the size of outside dimensions of the flask.

Rough boards or bottom boards of same size should be provided, one for each mold that will be put up in a day.

Boards for snap work are made of from $\frac{7}{8}$- to 1-inch stuff, and should have two stiff cleats, as shown in Fig. 2, to hold them straight.

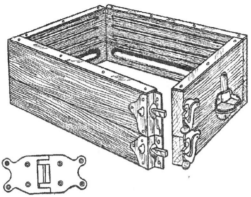
Fig. 1. Snap Flask

Wood Flask. For heavier castings where the molds are made on the floor, box flasks are used made of wood or iron.

In the jobbing shop, wood flasks are more economical, as they can more readily be altered to fit a variety of patterns, while in a foundry turning out a regular line of castings, iron flasks pay because they require less repair.

Wooden flasks of necessity receive hard usage in the shop and grow weaker each time they are used. They will burn more or less each heat; they receive rough usage when the mold is shaken out; and often the flasks must be stored where they are exposed to all kinds of weather. It is economy, therefore, to build wooden flasks heavier than would be necessary if they were always to be used in their new condition.

Fig. 3 shows the construction of a typical wooden flask; the sides project to form lifting handles; the ends are gained in to the sides. Through bolts, in addition to the nailing, hold the sides firmly. A

Fig. 2. Mold Board

detail of the pin is shown at *A*, and at *B* is a cast-iron rocker useful on flasks over 4 by 5 feet, to facilitate lifting and rolling over. The cleats make it a simple matter to alter crossbars. The crossbars should be not over 8 inches on centers. For more than 3-foot spans they should have short crossbars through the middle connecting the long ones. In flasks 4 feet and over there should be one or more iron crossbars and a $\frac{1}{2}$-inch through bolt with good washers to clamp the sides firmly to them.

FOUNDRY WORK

TABLE II
Sizes of Wooden Flasks

Flask Sizes (6 inches deep)	Material			
	Sizes		Arrangement	
	Sides (inches)	Cross-bars (inches)	Short Cross-bars (rows)	Iron Cross-bars (number)
Up to 24 by 24 in.	1½	1		
18 in. to 24 in. wide up to 5 ft. long	2	1		1
24 in. to 36 in. wide up to 6 ft. long	2½	1¼	1	2
36 in. to 48 in. wide up to 7 ft. long	3	1½	2	2

NOTE. For each additional 6-inch depth of cope or drag add 25 per cent to the thickness given.

Table II shows thickness of stuff for sides and crossbars for average sizes of jobbing flasks.

Illustrative Example. Find thickness of sides and bars in a flask 30 by 48 inches.

By referring to Table II, it is noted that for lengths on the sides over 2 feet and under 5 feet the thickness of *sides* should be 2 inches.

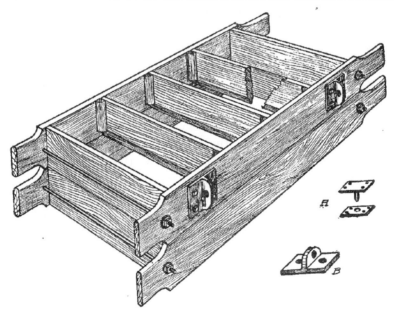

Fig. 3. Wooden Flask

Similarly, for widths of flask of over 24 inches and under 36 inches, the thickness of *crossbars* should be 1¼ inches.

Iron Flask. In Fig. 4 is shown the construction of a large iron flask suitable for dry-sand work. The pieces of the flask are usually cast in open sand from a skeleton pattern, all holes cored in. The crossbars are cast in the same way; they have a slot in the flange instead of holes to facilitate adjusting them. Trunnions and rockers are sometimes cast on the sides in a core instead of being made separate and bolted on. Holes for pins are usually drilled through the joint flange. For pins, short iron bars are used temporarily in

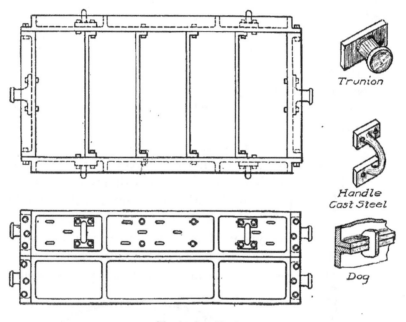

Fig. 4. Iron Flask

closing. The thickness of metal varies from $\frac{7}{8}$ inch to $1\frac{1}{4}$ inches, according to size of flask.

In Fig. 5 is shown a typical form of iron flask used on some molding machines. The boxes are cast in one piece. The handles serve as lugs for the closing pins. Only one pin is fixed on each box. This makes the boxes interchangeable and capable of being used for either cope or drag.

Shovel. For cutting and handling loose sand the molder uses a shovel with flat blade, as in Fig. 6, for it is often more convenient to let the sand slide off of the side of the shovel than off of the end.

FOUNDRY WORK

This is especially true when shoveling sand into bench molds or molding-machine flasks.

Sieve. The foundry sieve or riddle, Fig. 7, is used to break up and remove lumps, shot iron, nails, etc., from the sand placed next the pattern or joint. Sieves should have oak rims with brass or galvanized-iron wire cloth. In ordering, the diameter of rim and the number of meshes to the inch of the woven wire is given. Good sizes for the iron foundry are 16 inches to 18 inches diameter, No. 8 to 12 on bench work, No. 4 to 8 on floor work.

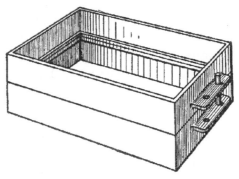

Fig. 5. Flask for Molding Machine

Rammers. Rammers are used for evenly and quickly packing the sand in the flask. One end is in the shape of a dull wedge, called the peen end, the other is round and flat called the butt end. Of the rammers shown in Fig. 8, a is the type used on bench work; b is a floor rammer having cast heads and wooden shaft; c shows a rammer made up in the foundry by casting the

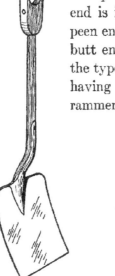

Fig. 6. Flat Blade Shovel

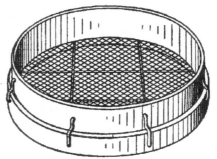

Fig. 7. Foundry Sieve

heads on the ends of an iron bar; d shows a small peen cast on a short rod—this is convenient for getting into corners or pockets on floor work.

Pneumatic Type. In shops equipped with compressed air a pneumatic rammer, as shown in Fig. 9, is sometimes used to butt off large flasks, and for ramming loam molds in pits.

Finishing Tools. Molders' tools are designed for shaping and slicking the joint surfaces of a mold and for finishing the faces of the mold itself. Excepting the trowels, they are forged in one piece

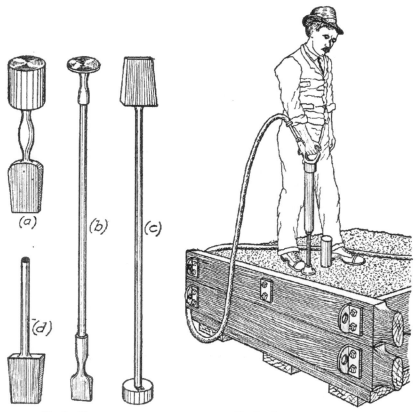

Fig. 8. Rammers   Fig. 9. Pneumatic Rammers

from steel. The trowels have steel blades and short round handles which fit conveniently into the grasp of the hand. All of the tools are ground slightly crowning on the bottom, and they are rocked just a little as they are worked back and forth over the sand to prevent the forward edge cutting into the surface of the mold.

Of the sixty or more combinations of shapes on the market, the few illustrated represent the ones most commonly used in jobbing shops.

Trowels. Trowels, Fig. 10, are used for shaping and smoothing the larger surfaces of a mold. The square trowel *a* is convenient for working up into a square corner, and the finishing trowels *b* and *c*

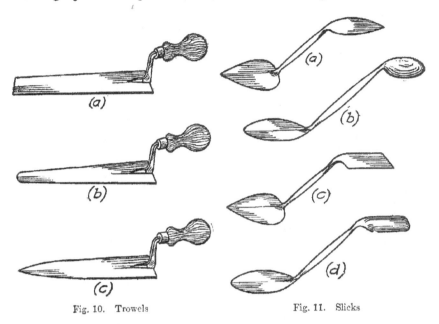

Fig. 10. Trowels   Fig. 11. Slicks

are more for coping out and finishing along the curved edges of a pattern. Trowels are measured by the width and length of blade.

Slicks. Slicks are designated by the shape of the blade and the width of the widest blade. In Fig. 11, *a* is a heart and leaf; *b* is a

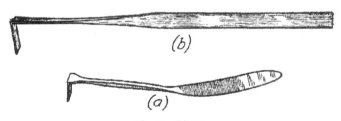

Fig. 12. Lifters

leaf and spoon; *c* is a heart and square; and *d* is a spoon and bead. These are in sizes of 1 inch to $1\frac{3}{4}$ inches. They are used for repairing and slicking small surfaces.

Lifters. Fig. 12 shows lifters used to clean and finish the bottom and sides of deep narrow openings; *a* is a floor lifter, made in sizes from ⅛- by 10-inch to 1- by 20-inch; b is a bench lifter, the sizes of which vary from $\frac{3}{16}$ inch to $\frac{3}{4}$ inch wide.

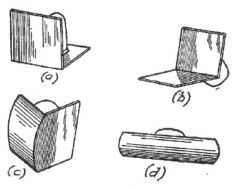

Fig. 13. Square Corner Slicks

Corner Slicks. Fig. 13 shows at a and b inside and outside square-corner slicks, made in sizes of 1 to 3 inches; c is a half-round corner, widths 1 inch to 2½ inches; and d is a pipe slick made 1 inch to 2 inches. This style of tool is mainly used on dry sand and loam work.

Swabs. Swabs are used to moisten the edges of the sand about a pattern before drawing it from the mold. This foundry swab is a dangerous though useful tool. Its danger lies in the too free use of water around the mold, which may result in blowholes. A good swab for bench work is made by fastening a piece of sponge, about double the size of an egg, to a goose quill or even a pointed hardwood stick. The point will act as a guide and the water may be made to run or simply drop from the point by varying the pressure on the sponge.

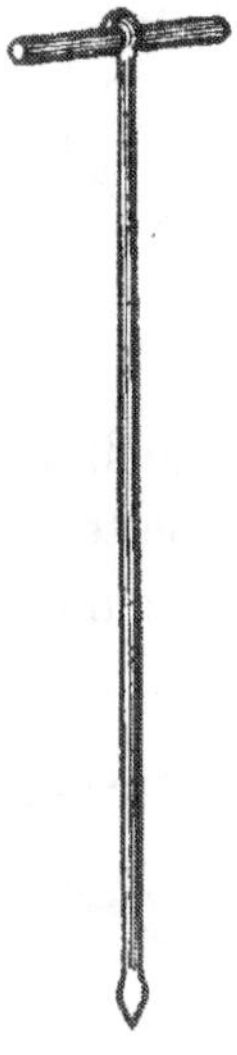

Fig. 14. Floor Swab

Floor swabs, Fig. 14, are made from hemp fiber. They should have a good body of fiber shaped to a point, and should be made about 12 inches or 14 inches long. They will take up considerable water and deliver it from the tip of the point. In heavy work the swab is trailed lightly over the sand like a long bristled brush.

Vent Rods. Vent wires are used to pierce small holes through the sand connecting the mold cavity with the outside air. For bench work a knitting needle is the most convenient thing to use. It should have a short hardwood handle or cast ball on one end. Select a needle as small as possible, so long as it will not bend when using it.

Fig. 15. Vent Rod

FOUNDRY WORK

Heavy vent rods are best made, as shown in Fig. 15, of a spring steel from $\frac{3}{16}$ inch to $\frac{1}{2}$ inch with the pointed end enlarged a little to give clearance for the body of the rod when run deep into the sand.

Draw Sticks. Draw sticks are used to rap and draw patterns from the sand. In Fig. 16 are shown three kinds: *a* is a small pointed rod $\frac{1}{4}$ inch to $\frac{3}{8}$ inch in size, which gets its hold by simply driving it into the wood of the pattern; *b* is a wood screw welded to an eye for convenience; *c* is an eye rod with machine-screw thread, which requires a metal plate let into the pattern. The plate is called a *rapping plate* and is made with separate holes not threaded, into which a pointed rapping bar is placed when rapping the pattern, thus preserving the threads used for the drawbar.

Clamps. In pouring, the parts of a mold must be clamped by some method to prevent the pressure of the liquid metal from separating them, causing a run-out.

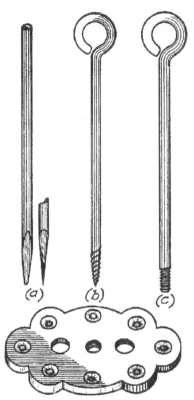

Fig. 16. Draw Sticks

For light work a weight such as shown in Fig. 17 is the most convenient. This is simply a plate of cast iron 1 inch to $1\frac{1}{2}$ inches thick, with a cross-shaped opening cast in it to give considerable liberty in placing the runner in the mold. The weights are from 15 to 40 pounds, according to size of flasks.

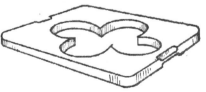

Fig. 17. Weight

Floor flasks are fastened with clamps made of cast iron which are tightened by prying them on to a hardwood wedge. In Fig. 18 is shown how the wedge may first be entered and how the clamping bar is used to firmly clamp the flask. For iron flasks used in dry-sand work the clamps are very short, as only the flanges are clamped together, as may be seen in Fig. 4. In that connection iron wedges are used instead of wood. Often the iron bottom board is clamped on and the joint flanges bolted together before pouring.

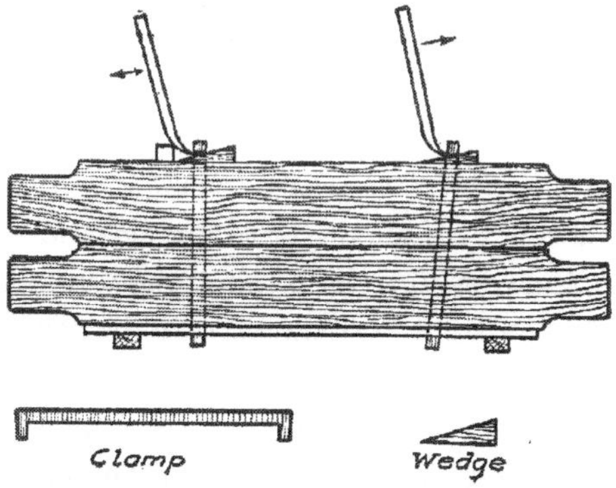

MOLDING PROCESSES
PRINCIPLES OF GREEN-SAND MOLDING

Good Work. There are certain principles underlying iron molding which hold good in all classes of founding, and a practical understanding of these principles is necessary for good work in any line.

Fig. 18. Illustrating Method of Clamping

Aside from the fact that generally a mold is wanted which takes the least possible time to put up, three things aimed at in green-sand work are: (1) a sound casting, which is free from internal imperfections, such as blow holes, porous spots, shrinkage cracks, etc.; (2) a clean casting, which is free from dirt, such as slag, sand, etc.; and (3) a smooth casting, having a uniform surface free from scabs, buckles, cold-shuts, or swells.

Sand Mixture. The natural sands best adapted to obtain these results have already been dealt with. The methods of adding new sands vary with different classes of work. For light work the entire heap should be kept in good condition by adding a little new sand every day, for the light castings do not burn out the sand to a great extent.

On heavier work of 50 pounds and upward, the proportion of sand next the pattern is so small compared with that used simply to fill the flask, that it does not pay to keep the entire heap strong enough for actual facing. The heap should be freshened occasionally with a cheap molding sand, but for that portion of the mold which forms the joint surface, and especially that which comes in contact with the metal, a facing sand should be used.

The range of new sand in facing mixtures on a 10-part basis, with sea coal in addition, is as tabulated herewith:

Proportions of Facing Mixtures

(Basis of 10 Parts)

Sand			Sea Coal (additional part)
New	Old	Free	
3—6	6—2	1—2	$\frac{1}{6}$—$\frac{1}{8}$

These proportions, and the thickness of the layer of facing sand, vary with the weight of metal in the casting. Too much new sand tends to choke the vent and to cause sand to cake; too little new sand renders facing liable to cut or scab. Too much sea coal makes sand brittle and more difficult to work, and also gives off too much gas which is liable to cause blowholes in casting. Not enough sea coal allows the sand to cake, making cleaning difficult.

Tempering and Cutting. To prepare foundry sand for making a mold, it must be tempered and cut through. This is now usually done by laborers. To temper the sand, throw water over the heap in the form of a sheet by giving a peculiar backward swing to the pail as the water leaves it. Then cut the pile through, a shovelful at a time, letting the air through the sand and breaking up the lumps. This moistens the clay in the sand, making it adhesive and puts the pile in the best condition for working.

To test the temper, give one squeeze to a handful of sand. An excess of water will at once be detected by the soggy feeling of the sand. Now hold the egg-shaped lump between thumb and finger of each hand and break it in the middle. The edges of the break should remain firm and not crumble. Too much moisture will make excess of steam in the mold, causing blowholes. Not enough moisture renders sand weak and apt to wash or cut.

Bearing in mind the nature of the materials we have to work with, we must now study the important operations involved in making a sand mold.

Sifting. The sand next to the joint and over the pattern should be sifted. The thickness of this layer of sifted sand varies from about $\frac{3}{4}$ inch for light work to 2 inches on very heavy work. The fineness of the sieve used depends upon the class of work. No. 16 or 12 would be used for small name plates, stove plate, etc., while

No. 8 or 6 is good for general machinery work. On floor work, from 4 to 6 inches of sand back of the facing should be riddled through a No. 4 sieve to ensure more even ramming and venting.

Ramming. The object of ramming is to make the sand hang into the flask and to support the walls of the mold against the flow and pressure of the metal. The knack of ramming just right only

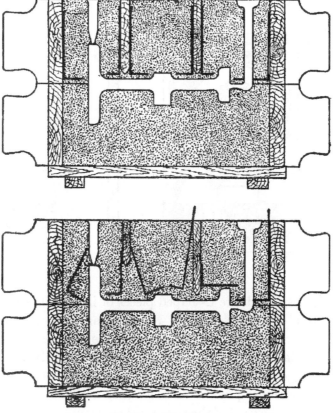

Fig. 19. Setting Gaggers

comes with continued practice and comparison of results. Hard ramming closes up the vent, causing blowholes. Iron will not "lay" into a hard surface. Soft ramming leaves a weak mold surface, and the flow of the metal as it enters the mold washes or cuts the sand, leaving a scab on one part of the casting and sand holes on another. A mold rammed too soft tends to swell under the pressure of the liquid metal, making the casting larger than the pattern or leaving an unsightly lump on the casting. The bottom parts of a mold, being under greater casting pressure, must be rammed somewhat harder than the upper portions. The joint also should be packed firmly, as it is exposed to more handling than any other part.

Gaggers. Crossbars are put in the cope to make it possible to lift the sand with the cope without excessively hard ramming. As an additional support for the cope sand on large work there are

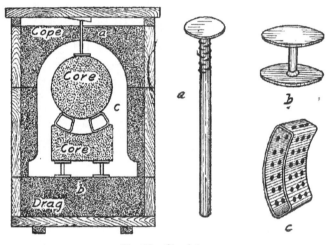

Fig. 20. Chaplets

used gaggers, which are L-shaped pieces of iron made from wrought or cast iron of from $\frac{5}{16}$-inch to $\frac{1}{2}$-inch square section.

The force of sand pressing against the long leg of the gagger holds it in place and the short leg supports the sand about it. Therefore the gagger will hold best when the long leg is placed tight against the crossbar and is plumb. The long leg of the gagger should not project above the level of the cope, as there is much danger of striking it and breaking in the mold after the flask is closed. In Fig. 19 are shown the right and wrong ways of setting gaggers.

Use of Chaplets. Chaplets should be used to support parts of cores which cannot be entirely secured by their prints which are held in the sand of the mold. In Fig. 20 are shown the three principal forms of chaplets used, and how they are set in the mold; *a* is a stem chaplet; *b* is a double-headed or stud chaplet; and *c* is a form of chaplet made up of strip metal.

That portion of the chaplets which is to be bedded in metal is tinned to preserve it from rusting, because rusty iron will cause liquid metal to blow. For small cores nails are often employed for this purpose, but only new ones should be used. With the stem chaplets the tails must be cut off when the casting is cleaned—the stud chaplet becomes entirely embedded in the metal. There are now manufactured and on the market many different styles of chaplets. In selecting the size and form for a given purpose the head of the chaplet should be large enough to support the weight of the core without crushing into the sand and thin enough to fuse into the liquid metal. The stem must be small enough to fuse well to the metal and stiff enough, when hot, not to bend under its load.

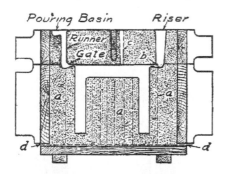
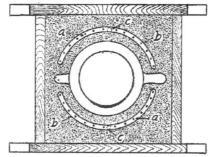

Fig. 21. Use of Risers

Venting. In the section on Sands reference has already been made to gases which must be taken off from a mold when it is poured. There are three forms of these: (1) air, with which the mold cavity is filled before pouring; (2) steam, formed by the action of the hot metal against the damp sand during the pouring process; and (3) gases formed while the casting is cooling, from chemical reactions within the liquid metal and from the burning of organic matter, facings, core binder, etc., in the sands of the mold. It is of the greatest importance that these gases pass off quickly and as completely as possible. If they do not find free escape through the mold they are forced back into the liquid metal, making it boil or blow. This may blow the metal out through risers and runners, or simply form numerous little bubble-shaped cavities in the casting, called *blowholes*. These often form just below the skin of the casting and are not discovered until the piece is partially finished.

FOUNDRY WORK

Various Systems. One cannot depend entirely upon the porosity of the molding sands, but must provide channels or vents for the escape of these gases. For light work a free use of the vent wire through the sand in the cope will answer all purposes.

On castings of medium weight, besides venting with the wire, risers are placed directly on the casting or just off to one side as shown in Figs. 19 and 21. These are left open when the mold is poured and provide mainly for the escape of the air from the mold.

Heavy castings that will take time to cool, and thus keep facings burning for a long time after the mold is poured, require venting on sides and bottom as well as top. Fig. 21 shows side vents *aaaa'* connecting with the air through the channel *bbb* cut along joint and risers *ccc* passing through the cope. At the bottom the vents connect with cross-vents *dd* run from side to side between the bottom board and edge of flask. Fig. 22 shows a mold bedded in the floor; the side or down vents connect at the top, as in previous examples, and at the bottom with a cinder bed about 2 inches thick, rammed over entire bottom of pit. The gases find escape from this cinder bed through a large gas pipe.

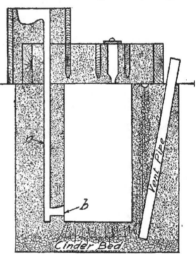

Fig. 22. Mold Bedded in Floor

Action During Pouring. In pouring, the gas from vents should be lighted as soon as may be. The burning at the mouths of vents helps to draw the gases from below and also keeps the poisonous gas out of the shop.

It is customary to keep risers closed with small cover plates when large castings are being poured so that the air in the mold will be compressed as the metal rises in the mold. This helps sustain the walls of the mold and forces the vents clear so that they will act more quickly when the mold is full. These covers are removed occasionally to watch the progress of pouring, and are entirely removed when the metal enters the risers.

Gating. *Gating* is the term applied to the methods of forming openings and channels in the sand by which liquid metal may enter the mold cavity. The terms *sprues* and *runners* are also used in the same connection in some shops.

Functions of Parts. There are practically three parts to all gates: pouring basin; runners; and gate, as seen in Fig. 21. The runner is formed by a wooden gate plug made for the purpose. The pouring basin is shaped by hand on top of the cope, and the gate proper is cut along the joint surface by means of a gate cutter. In all cases the gate section should be smaller than any other part so that, when pouring, the runner and basin may be quickly flooded; also that the gate when cold will break off close to the casting and lessen the work of cleaning.

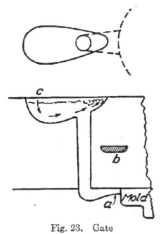

Fig. 23. Gate

The object of gating is to fill the mold cavity with clean metal—to fill it quickly, and while filling, to create as little disturbance as possible in the metal.

The impurities in liquid metal are lighter than the metal itself, and they always rise to the top when the melted metal is at rest or nearly so. Advantage is taken of this important property to accomplish the first of the objects mentioned.

Fig 23 shows a good type of gate to use on light work. For reasons given, the point a should have the smallest sectional area. This section should be wider than it is deep as shown at b, because the hot iron necessary for light work runs very fluid.

The runner should not be more than $\frac{5}{8}$ to $\frac{3}{4}$ inch in diameter. The pouring basin should be made deepest at point c, and slant upward crossing the runner. When pouring, the stream from the ladle should enter at c, flood the basin at once, and keep it in this condition. The current of the metal will then tend to hold back the slag, allowing clean metal to flow down the runner.

Skimming Gate. When particularly clean castings of medium weight are required, some form of skimming gate should be used. Fig. 24 illustrates one of several practical forms. They all depend for their efficiency upon the principle cited. In the illustration, *a* is the pouring basin and runner, *b* is a good sized riser placed about 3 or 4 inches from *a*, and *c* is a channel cut in the cope joint, connecting these two. The gate *d* should be cut in the drag side of the joint, just under the riser but at a right angle with the direction of *c*. The metal rushing down the runner is checked by the small size of the gate and so washes any dirt or slag up into the large riser *b*. The level of metal in this riser must be sustained by sufficiently rapid pouring until the mold is filled.

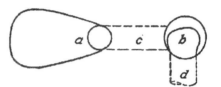

In bench work and floor work, the greatest care must be used to have all parts of the gate absolutely free from loose sand or facing which would wash into the mold with the first flood of metal.

On heavy work special skimming gates are not used, for the capacity of the pouring basin is very much greater than that of the runners which can be quickly flooded and thus retain the slag. Besides this, large risers are set at the sides

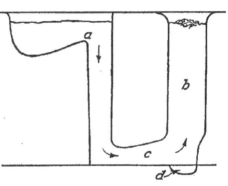

Fig. 24. Skimming Gate

or directly upon the casting, to receive any loose sand or facing that washes up as the mold is being filled. Fig. 22 illustrates this type.

Important Conditions. As regards the filling of the mold quickly and quietly, these two conditions are closely allied. The shape and thickness of the casting are the important factors in determining the number and position of the gates. Aside from the fact that the gate should never be heavier than the part of the casting to which it attaches, the actual size of the gate opening is something that the molder must learn from experience.

In arranging gates with regard to the shape of the pattern, the following points should be borne in mind: Place gates where the natural flow of the metal will tend to fill the mold quickly. Usually gate on the lighter sections of the casting. Select such points on the casting that the gates may be broken and ground off with least trouble—the greater the number of castings to be handled, the more important this point becomes. A study of the molding problems given will illustrate this point.

Provide enough gates to fill all parts of the mold with metal of uniform temperature. This depends upon the thickness of the work, as is illustrated in Fig. 25 by two molds having the same shape at the joints but of different thicknesses. In thin castings the metal tends to chill quickly, so it must be well distributed. In this illustration, a is a plate $\frac{1}{4}$ inch thick, and should have several gates. A piece having the same diameter but heavier, would run better from one gate as at b, while if a bushing of this diameter is required, the best results would be obtained by gating near the bottom, as in Fig. 22. For running work at the bottom as shown in Fig. 22, the gate piece b is separate from the runner, and is slicked into the mold after the pattern is drawn. The runner r should extend below the level of the gate to receive the force of the first fall of metal, which otherwise would tend to cut the sand of the gate.

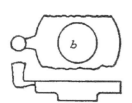

Fig. 25. Use of Gates

Fig. 26. Sinking of Casting

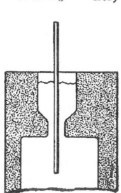

Fig. 27. Feeding Rod

Shrinkage Heads. Melted metal shrinks as it cools, and this process begins from the moment the mold is filled. The surfaces next to the damp sand are the first to solidify, and they draw to themselves the more fluid metal from the interior. This process goes on until the whole casting has solidified. This shrinkage causes the grain in the middle to be coarse and sometimes even open or porous.

The lower parts of a casting are under the pressure or weight of all the metal above, and so resist these shrinkage strains. The top parts, however, require the pressure of liquid metal in gates or risers to sustain them until they have hardened sufficiently to hold their shape, or they will sink as indicated by the section, Fig. 26. Risers, mentioned in connection with securing clean metal, are also required on heavy pieces to prevent this distortion and to give sound metal. When used in this way they are called *shrinkage heads* or *feeders*. They should be 6 or 8 inches in diameter, so as to keep the iron liquid as long as possible, and should have a neck 2 or 3 inches in diameter, to reduce the labor required to break them from the casting in cleaning. To prevent the metal in this neck from freezing, an iron feeding rod is inserted, as in Fig. 27, and is churned slowly up and down. This insures fluid metal reaching the interior. As the level in the feeder lowers, hot metal should be added from a hand ladle.

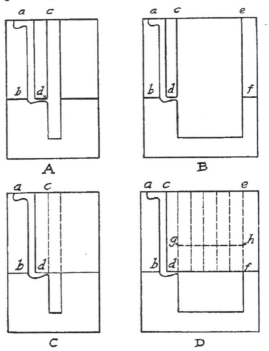

Fig. 28. Illustrating Pressure of Liquids in Molds

Pressure in Molds. The subject of the pressure of liquid iron mentioned repeatedly in the foregoing pages, must be dealt with by the molder, in weighting his copes, strengthening flasks, securing cores, etc., and most frequently in connection with the first of these.

Natural Laws. Molten iron acts in accordance with the same natural laws that govern all liquids—as, for example, water (see Mechanics, Part II); iron, however, is 7.2 times heavier than water. The two laws applicable in foundry work are these: (1) Liquids always seek their own level; (2) pressure in liquids is exerted in every direction.

Pressure-Head Example. Applying the first law, if we have two columns of liquid iron connected at the bottom, they would just balance each other. For convenience we shall leave out of our calculations the upward pressure on the gates in the following examples, for in practical work they need seldom be taken into account.

In *A*, Fig. 28, suppose these columns stand 6 inches above the joint *bd*, and that the column *cd*, has an area of 1 square inch. In *B*, suppose the area of the right-hand column *cdef* is 5 times the area of column *cd*. In both cases the level with top of runner *a* will be maintained. The depth of the cavity below the joint *bdf* makes no difference in maintaining these levels. The weight of one cubic inch of iron, .26 pound, is taken as the basis of all calculations.

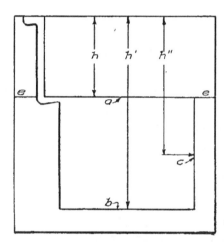

Fig. 29. Diagram Showing Analysis of Liquid Pressure

Now if we close the column *cd* at *d*, as in *C*, it is clear that it would require the actual weight of that column to balance the lifting pressure of the surface *d*, or $6 \times .26 \times 1 = 1.56$ pounds. And if the larger area *df* is closed over, as in *D*, it takes 5 times this weight to resist the pressure exerted upon it by the runner, or $6 \times .26 \times 5 = 7.8$ pounds. If the pattern projected 2 inches into the cope, the height of the runner above the surface acting against the cope would be 4 inches, and the pressure to be overcome would be equal to the weight of *cghe*, or $4 \times .26 \times 5 = 5.2$ pounds.

The important factors, then, are: height of runner; and area of mold which presses against the cope. We can therefore state a rule: *To calculate the upward pressure of molten iron, multiply the depth in inches by the weight of one cubic inch of iron (.26), and multiply this product by the area in square inches upon which the pressure acts.*

Pressure-Distribution Example. Applying the second law cited, the strains on sides and bottom of molds and upon cores is explained.

By the rule just stated we first find the pressure per square inch at any given level by multiplying the depth by .26, and it is obvious that this pressure increases, the lower in the mold a point is taken.

In Fig. 29, the pressure at a equals $h \times 26$. This also acts against the sides at ee. The pressure at b is $h' \times .26$, and is exerted sidewise and downward. The pressure at c is $h'' \times 26$. This point, being half way between the levels a and b, represents the average sidewise or lateral pressure on all of the sides.

If this mold, then, is 11 inches square and 9 inches deep, with the pouring basin 6 inches above the joint, we have the following conditions:

Area of a	= 121 sq. in.
Area of b	= 121 sq. in.
Area of c (one side)	= 99 sq. in.
Area of four sides	= 396 sq. in.
Height of h = 6 in.;	pressure head = 1.56 lb. per sq. in.
Height of h' = 15 in.;	pressure head = 3.90 lb. per sq. in.
Height of h'' = $10\frac{1}{2}$ in.;	pressure head = 2.73 lb. per sq. in.

Multiplying these together, we have the pressures on the various faces as follows:

Upward pressure on a	= 188.76 lb.
Total pressure on side c	= 270.27 lb.
Total pressure on four sides	= 1081.08 lb.
Total downward pressure on b =	471.90 lb.

A study of these figures shows the necessity of well-made flasks and bottom boards, for these must resist a greater pressure even than that required to keep the cope from lifting. They also show clearly why the lower parts of the casting resist the pressure of the gases more and require firmer ramming then the upper portions.

Variation of Pressure Head. A difference in the way a pattern is molded may make a great difference in the weight required on the cope. Compare A and B, Fig. 30. Supposing this pattern is cylindrical in shape and with the dimensions as indicated, we would have the following basis:

Area of circle a = 113.10 sq. in.
Area of circle b = 78.54 sq. in.
Area of ring $c'c'$ (b subtracted from a) = 34.56 sq. in.

Then

Total lift on cope A is $8 \times .26 \times 113.10$ = 235.24 lb.

The lift on cope B is $8 \times .26 \times 34.56 = 71.88$
$+ (8+5) \times .26 \times 78.54 = 265.46$

Total lift on B = 337.34 lb.

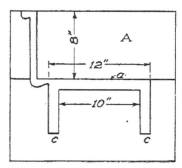 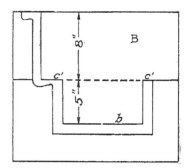

Fig. 30. Diagram Showing Difference in Pressure on Cope Due to Placing of Pattern

Variation of Pressure Distribution. Fig. 31 is an example of a core 5 inches square surrounded by 1 inch of metal, with a runner 6 inches high. We have here:

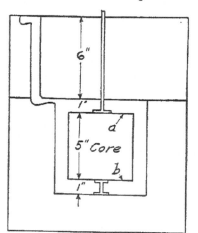

Fig. 31. Diagram Showing Difference in Pressure on Top and Bottom of a Cube

Pressure per square inch on a is $7 \times .26 = 1.82$ lb.

Pressure per square inch on b is $12 \times .26 = 3.12$ lb.

The difference in these pressures is 1.30 pounds per square inch. Then for every foot of length in the core we must balance a lifting pressure on the bottom of the core of $5 \times 12 \times 3.12 = 187.2$ pounds, until the metal covers surface a, when it will exert a counteracting downward pressure, and the strain on the chaplets will be only $5 \times 12 \times 1.30 = 78$ pounds.

FOUNDRY WORK

Common Defects in Castings. Some of the ordinary defects which the beginner will find on his castings are as follows:

Short Pourings. The amount of metal in the ladle is misjudged with the result that the mold is not completely filled.

Blowholes. These come from gases becoming pocketed in the metal instead of passing off through the sand. This is due to hard ramming, wet sand, etc.

Cold-Shuts. These form when two streams of metal chill so much before they meet, that their surfaces will not fuse when forced against each other, as illustrated in Fig 32.

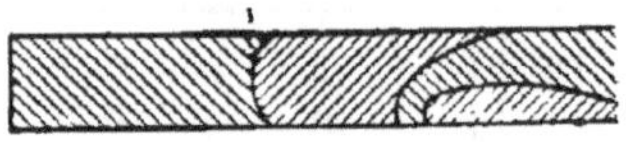

Fig 32 Cold-shuts

Sand Holes. These come from the washing of loose sand or excess of facing into the mold cavity when pouring. They are usually bedded in the cope side of the casting.

Scabs. Scabs show like small warts or projections on the surface of the casting. They result from small patches of the mold face washing off. They may be caused from too much slicking, which draws the moisture to the surface of the mold, making the skin flake under the drying effect of the incoming metal.

Swells. Swells are bulged places on a casting and are due to soft ramming which leaves the walls of the mold too soft to withstand the pressure of the liquid metal.

Shrinkage Cracks. These are due to unequal cooling in the casting. They are sometimes caused by the mold being so firm that it resists the natural shrinkage of the iron, causing the metal to pull apart when only partially cold.

Warping. This occurs when these strains cause the casting to bend or twist, but are not sufficient to actually crack the metal.

TYPICAL MOLDING PROBLEMS

General Precautions. When starting to ram a flask, see that the sands to be used are well cut through and properly tempered. Select a flask large enough to hold the pattern and have at least 2 inches clear of the flask all around for bench work, and 4 to 8 inches on floor molds, depending upon the weight of the work to be cast. See that the flask is strong enough to carry the sand without racking and that the pins fit. Have the necessary tools at hand, such as sieve, rammer, slicks, etc.

Jointing. Examine the pattern to be molded to see how it is drafted and note especially how the parting line runs. That part of the mold forming the surface between the parts of the flask is called the *joint*, and where it touches the pattern this joint must be made to correspond with the parting line.

The joint of a mold may be a plane or flat surface, or it may be an irregular one. When the joint is a flat surface it is formed entirely by the mold board except with work bedded in the floor; there it is struck off level with a straightedge. When it is irregular the drag joint must be *coped out* for every mold needed, that is, shaped freehand by the molder before making up the cope; or, by another method, the shape of the cope joint is built up first in a *match frame* with the cope part of the pattern bedded into it, and upon this form the drag may be packed repeatedly, receiving each time the desired joint surface without further work on the molder's part.

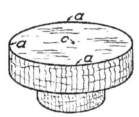

Fig. 33. Faceplate

Our first problems in molding illustrate these three methods of making the joint. It is aimed to give the directions for making up molds in as concise a form as possible. The student should refer frequently to the preceding sections and familiarize himself with the reasons underlying each operation.

Flat Joint. In the small faceplate shown in Fig. 33, all of the parting line *aaa* will touch the mold board, so the joint will be flat. The draft is all in one direction from the cope side *c*, therefore all of the pattern will be in the drag. Use a snap flask for this piece.

Molding Drag. Place a smooth mold board upon the bench or brackets. Place the drag with sockets down upon this. Set the pattern a little to one side of the center to allow for the runner. Sift sand over this about 1½ inches deep. Tuck the sand firmly around the pattern and the edges of the flask as indicated by the arrows in Fig. 34, using the fingers of both hands and being careful not to shift the sand away from the pattern at one point when tucking at another.

Fill the drag level full with well-cut sand. With the peen end of the rammer slanted in the direction of the blows, ram first around the sides of the flask to ensure the sand hanging in well, as at *1* and *2* in Fig. 35. Next carefully direct the rammer around the pattern, as at *3*, *4*, and *5*. Do not strike closer than 1 inch to the pattern with the end of the rammer.

Shifting the rammer to a vertical position, ram back and forth across the flask in both directions, being especially careful not to strike the pattern nor to ram too hard immediately over it. The student must judge by feeling when this course is properly rammed. Now fill the drag heaping full of sand. Use the butt end of the rammer around the edges of the

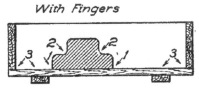

Fig. 34. Molding Sand with Fingers

flask first, then work in toward the middle until the sand is packed smooth over the top. With a straightedge strike off the surplus sand to a level with the bottom of flask. Take a handful of sand and throw an even layer about $\frac{1}{4}$ inch deep over the bottom of the mold. On this loose sand press the bottom board, rubbing it slightly back and forth to make it set well. With a hand at each end, grip the board firmly to the drag and roll it over. Remove the mold board and slick over the joint surface with the trowel. Dust parting sand over this joint (burnt core sand is good on this work), but blow it carefully off of the exposed part of the pattern.

Set the wooden runner or gate plug about 2 inches from the pattern, as shown in Fig. 23, page 24.

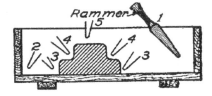

Fig. 35. Molding Sand with Rammer

In snap work the runner should come as near the middle of the mold as possible, to lessen the danger of breaking the sides, and to allow the weight to be placed squarely on top of the mold.

Molding Cope. Set the cope on the drag and see that the hinges come at the same corner.

Sift on a layer of sand about $1\frac{1}{2}$ inches deep. Tuck firmly with the fingers about the lower end of the runner and around the edges of the flask. Fill the cope and proceed with the ramming the same as for the drag.

Strike off the surplus sand, swinging the striking stick around the runner so as to leave a fair flat surface of sand. Partially shape a pouring basin as illustrated in Fig. 23, with a gate cutter, before removing the runner. Draw the runner and finish the basin with a gate cutter and gently smooth it up with the fingers. Carefully moisten the edges with a swab and blow it out clean with the hand bellows.

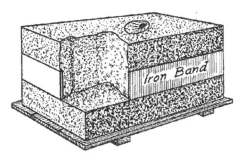

Fig. 36. Use of Iron Band

Lift the cope and repair any imperfections on the mold surface with the trowel or slicks. See that the sand is firm around the lower end of the runner. Blow through the runner and all over the joint to remove all loose parting sand. Slick over the sand which forms the top surface of the gate, between the runner and the mold.

Having finished the cope, moisten the sand about the edges of the pattern with a swab. Drive a draw spike into the center of the pattern and with a mallet or light iron rod, rap the draw spike slightly front and back and crosswise. Continuing a gentle tapping of the spike, pull the pattern from the sand. If any slight break occurs, repair it with bench lifter or other convenient slick. Cut the gate and smooth it down gently with the finger; blow the mold out clean with the bellows. No facing is needed if the castings

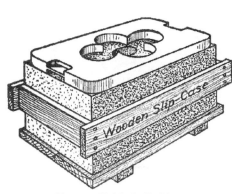

Fig. 37. Weight in Position

are to be pickled. The mold should now be closed and the snap flask removed.

Strengthening against Pressure. There are two methods used to strengthen these molds against the casting pressure. One is to use an iron band which will just slip inside of the flask before the mold is packed, as in Fig. 36. The other is to slide a wooden slip case over the mold after the snap flask is removed, as in Fig. 37. In either case the weight, shown in position in Fig. 37, should not be placed on the mold until pouring time, lest by its continued pressure it might crush the sand.

Coping Out. The second type of joint surface mentioned above is illustrated by the method of molding the tailstock clamp shown in Fig. 38. This is a solid pattern and rests firmly upon the mold board on the edges aa, but the parting line bbb runs below these edges. The bulk of the pattern drafts down from this line and so will be molded in the drag, while all above it will be shaped in the cope.

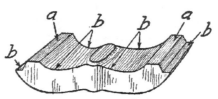

Fig. 38. Tailstock Joint

To mold the piece, set the pattern on the mold board, planning to gate into one end. Ram the drag, and roll it over, as described in the last example. With the blade of the trowel turned up edgewise, scrape away the sand to the depth of the parting line, bringing the bevel up to the main level of the joint, about $2\frac{1}{2}$ inches from the pattern, as shown at Fig. 39, and slick this surface smooth with the

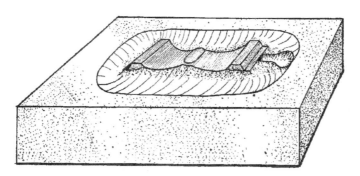

Fig. 39. Coped-Out Mold

finishing trowel or leaf and spoon. This process is called *coping out*. Dust parting sand on the joint thus made. Be careful not to get too much at the bottom of the coping next the pattern. Pack the cope, then lift it, and finish the mold as directed.

Shape of Draft. In coping out, the molder practically shapes the draft on the sand of the drag. Aim to have the lower edge of the coping parallel with the main joint for a short distance, and then spring gradually up to it at about the angle shown in the section at c, Fig. 40, as this is the strongest shape for the sand. If made with an abrupt angle as in d, the cope sand will tend to wedge into the cut with the danger of a drop or break when the cope is lifted.

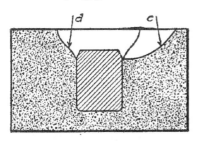

Fig. 40. Angle of Joint

In many cases, more especially in floor work, an abrupt coping angle may be avoided as follows: Set wooden strips, whose thickness is equal to the depth of the desired coping, under the edges of the drag when ramming up the pattern. (Use, for example, the hand wheel

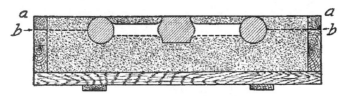

Fig. 41. Molding a Hand Wheel

shown in Pattern Making, Fig. 114.) When the drag is rolled over, the sand will be level with the top of strips and pattern at aa, Fig. 41. Remove the strips and strike surplus sand off level with edges of drag bb, and slick off the joint. Proceed with the cope in the usual manner. In gating this pattern, and wheels generally, place a small runner directly on the hub.

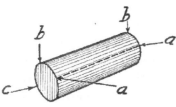

Fig. 42. Solid Bushing

Sand Match. The solid bushing, Fig. 42, serves to illustrate the use of a sand match. For exercise work, use only one pattern.

In practice, however, several small patterns are bedded into the same match. It is clear that in this pattern the parting line runs along the center of the cylinder, and to make a safe lift for the cope it should follow around the circumference of the ends *abc*, as shown by the heavy lines.

The frame for the match is shallow, and of the same size as the snap flask with which it is used. It is provided with sockets to engage the pins of the flask. The bottom board is fastened on with screws.

Fill the match with sifted sand rammed hard. Strike off a flat joint and bed in the pattern. Cope out the ends to the lower edge of the pattern, as shown in Fig. 43, flaring it well in order to make a good lift. Slick the whole surface over smooth. Rap and lift the pattern to test the correctness of the work.

Replace the pattern. Dust on parting sand and ram the drag, tucking carefully in the pocket at each end. Roll the two over. Lift off the match, and set it to one side. The pattern remains

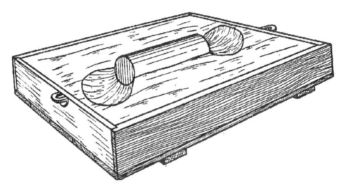

Fig. 43. Use of Sand Match

in the drag. Dust on parting sand. Set the runner and ram the cope as described. When the mold is opened and the pattern is drawn, it should be set back immediately into the match, ready for use again.

Usage. On account of economy of construction in the pattern shop, irregularly shaped work is often made in one piece. The molder must then decide whether it is cheaper to cope out each joint or to make up a sand match. Where the number of castings required is small, or where the pattern is large, it is better to cope out. But where a number of castings is required it is cheaper to make up a sand match. For methods of making quantities of castings and the use of a more permanent match, see the section on Duplicating Castings.

38 FOUNDRY WORK

In the foregoing the main use of the match was to save time. It frequently happens that a pattern is so irregular in shape that it will not lie flat on the board in any position. In this case, a match is absolutely necessary before the drag can be packed. For large patterns, the cope box of the flask is used to bed the pattern into instead of a separate frame. After the drag has been packed upon it and rolled over, this first cope is dumped, and the box repacked

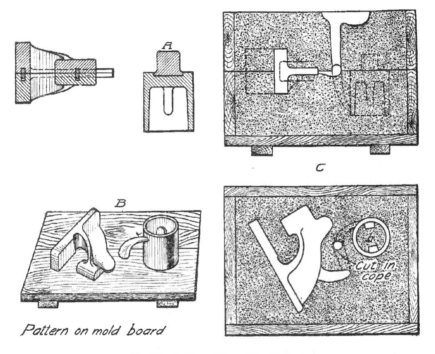

Fig. 44. Split- and Loose-Piece Patterns

with the necessary gaggers, vents, runners, etc., required for casting. The first cope is then termed, not a match, but a *false cope*.

For very light wooden patterns which may or may not have irregular parting lines, the pattern-maker builds up wooden forms to support the thin wood while the drag is being packed and to give the proper joint surface to the sand. This board serves exactly the same purpose as the sand match and false cope, but it is termed a *follow board*. See article on Pattern-Making.

Split=Pattern Molds. So far the patterns used have been made in one piece, but a flat joint is the most economical for the molder, when many castings are required. Generally such pieces as bushings, pipe connections, and symmetrical machine parts are made in halves; one piece of the pattern remaining in each part of the flask when the mold is separated. There are many cases, too, where, to make a flat joint for the mold, the pattern maker can separate one or more projections so as to have the main part of the pattern in the drag and to let these loose parts lift off in the cope.

The small punch frame and the gas-engine piston, shown in Fig. 44, are examples of these two classes of patterns. At A, the sections through the patterns show the methods of matching them together. B shows the drag parts of the patterns in position for molding. At C, is the section through the mold and the plan of the drag showing how the gates are connected. Attention is directed to the use of the horn sprue—the sprue pattern is shown at a—by which the metal enters the mold at the bottom. If the gate were cut at the joint surface, there would be danger of cutting the sand on top of the green-sand core b as the metal flowed in upon it.

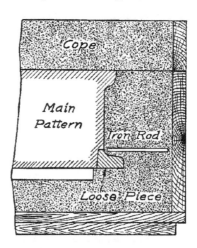

Fig. 45. Strengthening Mold with Iron Rod

Loose-Piece Mold. It often happens that bosses or projections are required on a casting at right angles to the main draft lines of the pattern and below the joint surface. Examples of such cases are shown in Pattern-Making. In molding such work, care must be taken that the overhanging portion of sand shall be strong enough to support itself. Where the projection is deep, the mold should be strengthened by nails or rods, as shown in Fig. 45. These should be wet with clay wash and set into the sand, when the mold is rammed.

Use of Green-Sand Core. Some work has projections on it which lie above or below the parting line in such a way that it cannot be molded by either of the foregoing methods. Examining the patterns for some of this work, we find two entire parting lines with the pattern made to separate between the two. Such patterns require between the drag and cope an intermediate body of sand, from the top and bottom of which the two parts may be drawn. In small work, as illustrated by the groove pulley, this intermediate form is held in place by the sand joint of the cope and drag, and is termed a *green-sand core*. The method of molding

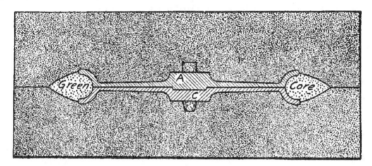

Fig. 46. Section of Mold

such a piece is given in Pattern-Making, Part I. To provide for pouring the casting, a runner should be placed on the hub of the first part packed *C*, Fig. 46, which shows a section of the mold before either part of the pattern has been removed. When the flask is rolled over to remove the final part *C* of the pattern, the runner is on top ready for pouring.

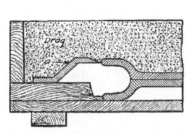

Fig. 47. Part Section of Mold Showing Use of Core-Lifting Ring

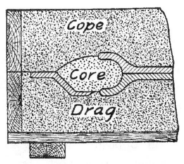

Fig. 48. Pattern Shown in Fig. 47 with Mold Complete

Core-Lifting Ring. Another method used does away with rolling the entire flask. A core-lifting ring is first cast slightly larger in diameter than the flange of the sheave, and having such a section as shown in *a*, Fig. 47. The ring is set in position in the middle of the inverted drag, the pattern is held central inside of the ring by the recess in the mold board. Pack the drag, roll over, and remove the mold board. Tuck the green core all around and slick off the top joint of the core. Pack the cope in the usual way, lift it off, and draw the cope pattern. Now, by means of lugs cast on this lifting ring, the green core may be lifted off of the drag pattern, allowing it to be removed. Replace the ring and close the cope; and the mold is complete, as shown in section, Fig. 48.

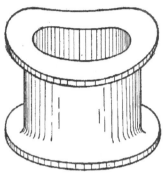

Fig. 49. Casting for Ten-Inch Nozzle

Three-Part Mold. In larger work, where the parting planes are farther apart, this intermediate body of sand is carried in a cheek part of the flask, and we speak of it as *three-part work.*

Fig. 49 shows a casting for a 10-inch nozzle, the mold for which illustrates this class of work. Here the pattern is separated just above the fillet of the curved flange. Fig. 50 gives a view of the mold, showing the way the joint is formed.

This casting should be made on the floor. Select a square flask, 4 inches on a side larger than the diameter of the flanges. The cheek should be as high as that part of the pattern which is molded in it. There should be two projecting bars on opposite sides of the cheek to support the sand, and crossbars in both drag and cope.

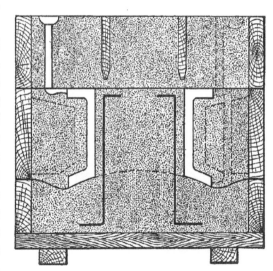

Fig. 50. Casting of a Nozzle

These should be well wet with clay wash before using the boxes.

Set the pattern centrally inside the cheek, and place a runner stick just the height of the pattern in one corner of this box. On account of the depth of the cheek, the sand must be rammed in two courses. Sift enough facing sand into the box to cover the joint and 5 inches up around the pattern to a depth of about $1\frac{1}{4}$

inches, tucking about the pattern with the fingers. Fill in about 5 inches of loose sand and before ramming tuck around the ends of the side bars, compressing the sand between the finger tips, having a hand on each side of the bar, as illustrated in Fig. 51. Now use the peen end of the floor rammer in the same general way as the hand rammer is used in bench molding. Guide the rammer around the sides of the flask and bars first, then direct it toward the bottom edges of the pattern. As the sand gradually feels properly packed at this level, direct the blows higher and higher up. Proceed in this way to within about 1 inch of the drag joint. Make this joint by ramming in sifted facing sand, being careful to tuck it firmly underneath the flange. Cope this joint to the shape of the curved flange.

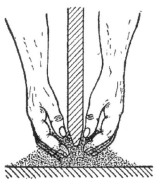

Fig. 51. Tucking Sand under Bars

Dust on parting sand. Place the drag in position and ram it up in the usual way, only using facing sand next the joint and pattern. Place six long gaggers to strengthen the sand which forms the inside of the casting. Clamp the drag to the cheek and roll them over. Test, repair, and dust parting sand on the joint. Try the cope. The bars should clear the pattern and joint by about 1 inch. Set the cope runner about 2 inches to one side of the cheek runner and set the riser in the corner opposite. Sift on facing sand and tuck well with the fingers under the crossbars. Shovel in well-cut sand and finish packing the cope. Form a pouring basin, and vent well. Lift the cope. Draw the pattern from the cheek. Join the runners on the cope joint and connect the mold with the riser. Lift the cheek and repair it. Draw the drag pattern. All of the mold surfaces should have black lead facing brushed over them with a camel's hair brush, and this facing slicked over. Cut a gate on the drag joint. Close the check on the drag. Close the cope on the cheek, and the mold is ready for clamping.

Floor Bedding. Owing to the development of the electric crane, there is much large work now rammed in iron flasks and rolled over, which was formerly always bedded in the floor. This method is still much used in jobbing shops to avoid making a complete large flask.

FOUNDRY WORK 43

The mold shown in Fig. 52 illustrates the principal operations involved. The casting is a flask section for a special steel-ingot mold, and in design is simply a heavy plate braced on one side by flanges and ribs of equal thickness. For convenience in ramming between

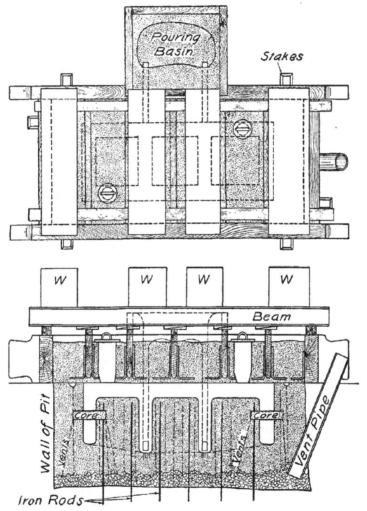

Fig. 52. Casting of Flask Section

the flanges, portions of the top plate of the pattern are left loose, as seen in Fig. 53.

Pit. Dig the pit for the mold 10 inches larger on each side than the pattern, and about 6 inches deeper. Having screened some hard cinders through a No. 2 riddle, cover the bottom of the pit with them to a depth of 3 inches. Ram these over with a butt rammer, and at one end set a piece of large gas pipe. Put a piece of waste on the top of this to prevent its getting choked with sand. Ram a 3-inch course of sand over the cinder bed and strike it off

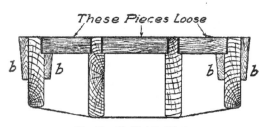

Fig. 53. Bedded-In Work

level at the depth of the pattern from the floor line. Sift facing sand over this where the pattern will rest; set the pattern, and with a sledge, seat it until it rests level. Remove the pattern and with the fingers test the firmness of packing all over the mold.

Vent these faces through to the cinder bed, and cover the vent holes with a ½-inch course of facing sand. Now replace the pattern, and bed it home by a few more blows of the sledge. The top of the pattern should now be level and flush with the floor line. Seat the runner sticks, and, to prevent the sand on the bottom of the runners from cutting, drive 10-penny nails about ¾ inch apart into this surface until the heads are flush. Ram the outside of the mold the same as if in a flask, and strike a joint on top. Ram

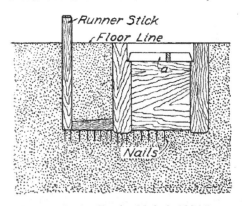

Fig. 54. Section Showing Method of Molding

green sand between the inside webs of the pattern, and strike off at the proper height with a short stick *a*, Fig. 54. Drive long rods 3 inches apart into these piers to pass through to solid sand below the cinder bed.

Vent all around the pattern, outside and inside, through to the cinder bed. On top of the inside piers cover these vent holes with facing sand, ram, and slick to finish; then cover with the loose pieces of the pattern.

Cope. Try the cope and stake it in place; set the risers and vent the plugs. Ram the cope, slicking off level for about 2 inches around the top of the risers, to receive a small iron cover.

FOUNDRY WORK 45

Lift the cope, repair, and face with graphite. Draw the pattern with the crane and finish the mold. Connect the outer vent holes by a channel with the vent plug. From the end of each core print *bbbb*, Fig. 53, vent through to the cinder bed, and set the cores. Close the cope. Set the runner box against the side of the cope and build a pouring basin with its bottom level with the top of the risers.

In weighting, great care must be exercised not to strain the cope. Place blocking upon the top ends of cope. Across these lay iron beams which will be stiff enough to support the load, and pile weights

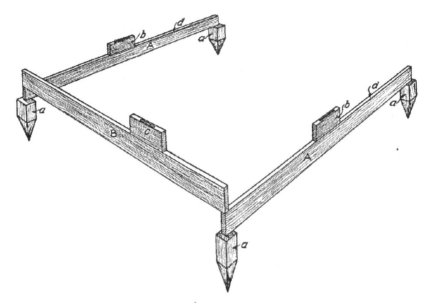

Fig. 55. Leveling a Bed for Open Sand Work

on these, as shown in Fig. 52. Now wedge under the beams to the crossbars of the cope at necessary points.

Open Mold. There is a large class of foundry rigging, such as loam plates, crossbars, and sides to iron flasks, which may be cast in open molds. As there is no head of metal, the beds must be rammed only hard enough to support the actual weight of the metal, or it will boil. To insure uniform thickness in the casting, the bed must be absolutely level.

Drive four stakes *aaaa*, as shown in Fig. 55, and rest the guide boards *AA* on the top of these. By using a spirit level *bb*, make these level, and bring them to the same height by testing with the straightedge B.

The space between the guide boards AA should be filled with well-cut sand even with their tops dd. Sift sand over the entire surface. Strike this sand off ⅜ inch higher than the guides, by placing a gagger under each end of the straightedge, as it is drawn over them. Tamp this extra sand to a level with the guides by rapping it down with the edge of the cross-straightedge, and the bed will be as shown in Fig. 56. We can now proceed to build up

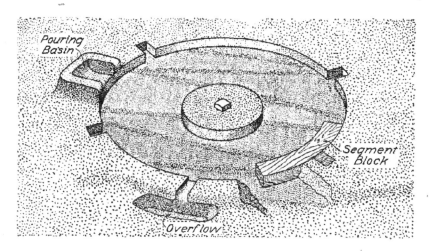

Fig. 56. Open Sand Mold

to a segment of pattern, or with a sledge drive a pattern into this surface.

The pouring basin should drain itself at the level of the top of mold, and an overflow may be cut on one edge to drain the casting to any desired thickness.

CORE WORK

Reference has been made in the first part of this article, under Divisions of Iron Molding, to the general difference between core work and green-sand work. This, and the section on Sands, the reader should review carefully.

Dry=Sand Cores

Materials. *Sand.* Here, as in green-sand molding, the principal material used is a refractory sand. In molding sand, however, the alumina or clay forms a natural bond in the sand. To meet the necessary requirements of cores we must use a naturally free sand as a base, and give it bond by adding some form of organic matter as a binder, then bake the core.

Binders. The most common binders are the following four materials: Ordinary *wheat flour* is an almost universal material for use as a core binder. Every one is familiar with its action when moistened and baked. The hard vegetable gum *rosin*—a by-product of the manufacture of turpentine—for use as a core binder, should be reduced to a powder. It melts under the heat of the oven, flows between the grains of sand, and upon cooling binds them firmly together. *Linseed oil*, made from flaxseed, acts in a way similar to rosin; a small proportion of oil together with some flour makes a very strong core. *Glue*, which is obtained from animal hoofs and from fish stock, is also used to some extent as a core binder. It should be dissolved in water before mixing with the sand.

Tempering. A weak *molasses water* is used for tempering the sand for small cores; and on the larger work the same purpose is served by *clay wash*. There are many patent combinations of the above or similar materials put on the market as *core compounds*. There are two classes of these: dry compounds, and liquid compounds. The advantages claimed for them is that they are more economical—(1) because a smaller proportion of the compounds is sufficient to obtain the desired results; and (2) because a large proportion of the sand may be used over and over again.

Reinforcement. Among other necessary core-room supplies are: annealed *iron wire* No. 6 to No. 16, and round *bar iron* in sizes $\frac{1}{4}$-inch, $\frac{3}{8}$-inch, $\frac{1}{2}$-inch, $\frac{5}{8}$-inch, and $\frac{3}{4}$-inch, which are cut to length as needed, and are bedded in the core sand to strengthen the core, as will be demonstrated later.

Venting. A supply of clean *cinders* must be available also for venting larger cores. Small *wax tapers* make good vents for crooked cores. There is also a *patented wax vent* for sale on the market.

Facing. As before stated, *charcoal* with some *graphite* is the principal facing material used on cores. It is always applied in liquid form by dipping the core or by using a flat brush having extra long bristles.

Equipment. *General Tools.* The general tools of the core room are similar to those already mentioned. A piece of iron rod very often replaces the regular rammer on account of the small size of the opening into which sand must be packed.

The trowel is the most common slick, because most of the surfaces which require slicking are flat ones formed by striking off after packing the box. Except in the largest work, the entire face of the core is not slicked over, so a variety small slicks is not needed.

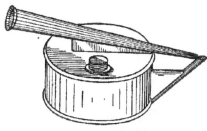

Fig. 57. Spraying Can

A spraying can, shown in Fig. 57, is used for spraying molasses water over small cores. Fill the can two-thirds full and blow into the mouthpiece.

Small cores are made up on a flat bench, the sand being in a small pile at the back. Larger boxes are rammed up on horses or on the floor, as is most convenient.

Baking. After being made up, cores are baked on core plates. The smaller plates are cast perfectly flat. Plates over 18 inches long are strengthened by ribs cast about 1 inch from the edge, as shown in Fig. 58; this keeps the plate from warping, and admits of its being picked up readily from a flat bench top or shelf.

Ovens are built with reference to the size of the cores to be baked. A good type of small oven is illustrated in Fig. 59. It can be run

Fig. 58. Core Plate

very economically with either coal or coke, and bakes cores up to 2 inches in diameter within half an hour. Each shelf is fastened to its own door, and, when open for receiving or removing cores, a door at the back of the shelf closes the opening. This prevents a waste of heat.

Fig. 60 shows the section through an oven suitable for the largest work, including dry-sand and loam molds. The fire box *A* is situated in one corner at the back; its whole top opens into the oven. At the floor level diagonally opposite is the flue *B* for conducting the

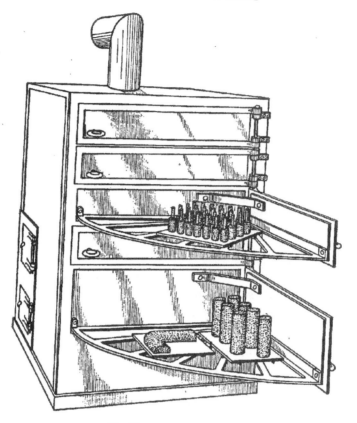

Fig. 59. Small Core Oven

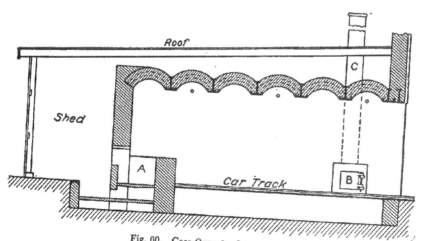

Fig. 60. Core Oven for Large Work

waste heat to the stack *C*. The entire front of the oven may be opened by raising the sheet-steel door. Two tracks side by side

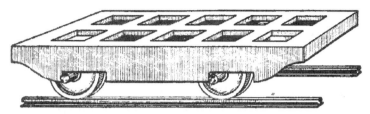

Fig. 61. Cast-Iron Car

accommodate cars upon which heavy work is run into the oven. Fig. 61 shows a good form of cast-iron car. The wheels are designed on the roller principle to make it easier to start the car when heavily loaded.

For medium work smaller ovens of this type are used. Racks similar to the one shown in Fig. 62 may be bolted on the sides, arranged to hold the ends of the core plates; and the car may carry a line of double racks to increase the capacity of the oven.

Conditions of Use. As mentioned before, cores form those parts of a mold which are to be nearly or entirely surrounded by metal; in other words, such parts as would be in danger of breaking or require too much work to be constructed in green sand. The object, then, in making cores is to insure a better casting and to reduce costs.

Cores are held in position by means of core prints (see Pattern-Making). The main weight of the core is supported by these prints and through them all vent must be taken off and all sand removed in cleaning. Therefore, cores must be stronger than green sand, because, whether large or small, they must stand handling while being set and must not cut or break during pouring.

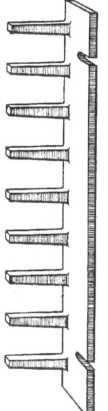

Fig. 62. Rack

They require greater porosity than green sand because their vent area is limited and their composition contains more gas forming material. Furthermore, cores must lose all their bond by the time the casting is cold, so that the sand may be easily removed no matter how small the available opening.

These conditions are obtained by using a coarse free sand and a binder. To give additional strength when necessary, iron wire or rods, or cast-iron core arbors are bedded in the core. These serve the same purpose in a core that the flask does in green-sand work.

Binder. The action of the binder enables the sand to retain its shape when the box is removed, and renders the core hard and strong when baked. In the mold the intense heat of the metal gradually burns out the organic matter or binder, leaving the core without bond. In this condition, the sand may readily be removed.

Too much binder tends to make the core sag out of shape before baking, and blow when metal strikes it; that is, give off more gas than the vents can carry away. With too little binder the sand does not bake hard, and cuts when the mold is poured.

The effectiveness of all binders, especially flour, depends upon their thorough mixing with the sand. The especial value of rosin and oil lies in the fact that by melting under the oven heat they form a more perfect bond with the sand.

Many intricate cores are now made with an oil mixture, without using rods or wires, which formerly were considered absolutely necessary for strength. Such cores must be well supported when green, must be thoroughly baked, and handled with much care until they are cold.

Core-Sand Mixture. No universal mixture for core sand can be given, as sands vary so much in different localities. The mixtures, as shown on the following page, illustrate approximate proportions.

In preparing core sand, the different ingredients should be measured out, thoroughly mixed, and sifted while dry. Temper the mixture a little damper than molding sand. Too much moisture makes the sand stick to the box. Not enough makes it hard to work and gives a crumbly surface if dried.

Facing. Blacking for light work should include one cup of molasses to a pail of water, into which is worked powdered charcoal until an even black coating is deposited upon the finger when dipped into the blacking and out again.

Core Mixtures

Materials	Small Cores (parts)	Large Cores (parts)	Intricate Smaller Cores (parts)	
Beach sand	10		15	15
Fire sand			15	
Molding sand				5
Sharp fire sand		8		
Strong loamy sand		2		
Flour	1	1½	1	2
Rosin			2	
Oil				1
Tempering means	Molasses water	Clay wash	Molasses water	

For heavy blacking there should be used about 2 parts charcoal and 1 graphite, mixed into thick clay wash.

Miscellaneous. In finishing small cores, they should be sprayed with weak molasses water while green, then well baked and removed from the oven. When cool enough to handle, they are dipped into the blacking; then put back in the oven until this facing has dried. For large cores the blacking is applied with a brush before baking.

All cores should be baked as soon as made, for air-drying causes the surface to crumble.

Cores must not be set in a mold while they are hot, or the mold will sweat, that is, beads of moisture will form on the inside faces. This would make the mold blow when poured.

A core should be rammed evenly and somewhat harder than a mold. Too hard ramming will make the sand stick in the box, besides giving trouble in casting. Too light ramming makes a weak core.

From the very nature of cores, the matter of venting them is very important and often calls for much ingenuity on the part of the core maker.

For simple straight work a good sized vent wire is run through before the box is removed. Half cores have their vents cut in each half before pasting together. Cinders are rammed in the center of large cores connecting through the prints, with the mold vents. For crooked cores, wax vents are rammed in the center—the wax melts away into the sand when the cores are baked, leaving smooth even holes. This is illustrated in one of the following examples.

FOUNDRY WORK

Methods of Making. The examples here given serve to illustrate the principal methods used in making cores.

Small Cylindrical Core. The simplest form of core is one which can be rammed up and baked as made by simply removing the box. Short bolt-hole cores, etc., are made in this way, as shown in Fig. 63.

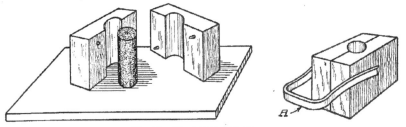

Fig. 63. Short Bolt-Hole Cores

Set the box on a flat bench top. Hold the two halves together by the clamp A. Ram the hole full of core sand by the use of a small rod. Slick off the top; run a good sized vent wire through the middle of the core. Remove the clamp. Set the box onto the core plate, rap the sides, and carefully draw them back from the core.

Symmetrical Shapes. Larger cylindrical cores, up to about 1½ inches diameter, are rammed in a complete box also, only they are rolled out on their sides, as shown in Fig. 64. This, however, tends to make a flat place on the side, from the weight of the sand supported on this narrow surface.

For this reason cylindrical cores of large diameter, and many symmetrical shapes, are made in half boxes. See Pattern-Making, Figs. 110, 208, 213, and 219. Such boxes are rammed from the open side. Wires are bedded when

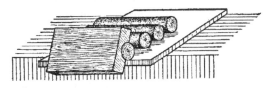

Fig. 64. Large Cylindrical Cores

necessary about in the middle of the half core. The fingers and the handle of a trowel are often used to ram the sand, and with the blade of the trowel the sand is struck off and slicked to the level of the top of the box.

When baked, two half cores are held with their flat sides together, and any slight unevenness in the joint removed by a gentle rubbing motion. A vent channel is then scraped centrally on each half. Paste, made of flour and molasses water, is applied around the edges and the two halves pressed firmly together; care is taken to see that they register all around. The core should then be placed in the oven to dry out the paste. When pasting cores of 6-inch diameter and over, it is well to bind the halves at each end with a single wrap of small wire.

Proper Seating. Wherever possible, core boxes should be made with their widest opening exposed for packing the core, and designed so that the core may rest, while being baked, on the flat surface formed by striking off at this opening.

Core plates will sometimes become warped. When a core would be spoiled by resting it directly upon such a plate, the unevenness is

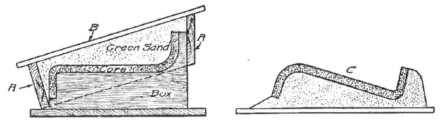

Fig. 65. Bedding a Crooked Core

overcome by sifting upon the plate a thin bed of molding sand and seating the core on this.

Crooked Shapes. All cores cannot be made with a flat surface for baking, as illustrated by a port core, the box for which is shown in Pattern-Making, Fig. 251. This core must be rolled over on a bed of sand. Using an oil mixture, ram the core carefully, bedding into it several wax vents. These should start near the end which will touch the main cylinder core and lead out of the end which will enter the chest core. To get this crooked core on a plate for baking, a wooden frame is roughly nailed together, which is large enough to slip over the core box when the loose pieces have been drawn off of the core, as shown in *A*, Fig. 65.

The space on top of the core is now filled with molding sand, rammed just enough to support the weight of the core. The edges of the frame project above the highest points of the core and form guides for striking off this sand and seating a core plate, as at *B*,

Fig. 65. Box, frame, and plate are now firmly clamped and rolled over, and the frame and box removed, leaving the core well bedded on the plate ready for the oven, as at *C*.

In manufacturing plants quantities of cores are often required which cannot be baked on a flat plate. To save the time and material necessary to roll each core onto a bed of sand, metal boxes are made, Pattern-Making, Figs. 233 and 234, and the core is baked in one part of the box. Only one casting is required of the larger portion of the box. The smaller part is duplicated for every core required for the day's mold.

Rod Reinforcing. Mention has been made of the use of wires for strengthening small cores. In making larger ones, there is a greater weight of sand to cause strain in handling the core, and proportionately greater casting strain. To resist these stresses a systematic network of rods is bedded in the core while being rammed, as shown in the sectional view, Fig. 66. Heavy

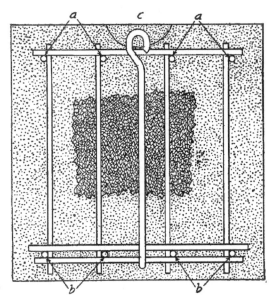

Fig. 66. Network of Rods in Cores

bars *aabb* extend the length of the core to give the main stiffness. Smaller cross-rods rest on these at the bottom and top, and with the small vertical rods tie the whole core together.

At even distances from each end lifting hooks *c* are placed. Cross-rods through the lower eyes of these hooks bring all the strain of the lift on the long heavy core rods. The holes in the top of the cores where the lifting hooks are exposed, are stopped off when the core is in the mold, by moistening the sides of the holes with oil and filling up with green sand.

Cinders are packed in the middles of such cores. They aid in drying the core. They furnish good vent, and they allow the sand to give when the casting shrinks, thus relieving the strain on the metal itself.

Use of Arbors. For the largest class of cores for green-sand work, cast-iron core arbors are used, of which a very satisfactory type is shown in Fig. 67. This consists of a series of light rings, A, carried on a cast-iron beam, B. The rings are of about $\frac{1}{2}$-inch metal cast in open sand and set about 8 inches on centers, and may be wedged to the beam. The beam has a hole at each end for lifting the core.

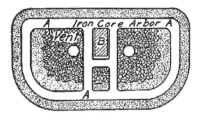

Fig. 67. Sections Showing Use of Cast-Iron Core Arbor

This skeleton is made up and tried in the box before the work of ramming the core is begun. It is then removed and given a coat of thick clay wash. A layer of core sand is first lightly rammed over the inside of the box, and the core arbor seated into this. The full thickness of core-sand facing is then firmly rammed, and the entire center filled with well-packed cinders. Vents through the facing at both ends provide for the escape of gases from these cinders.

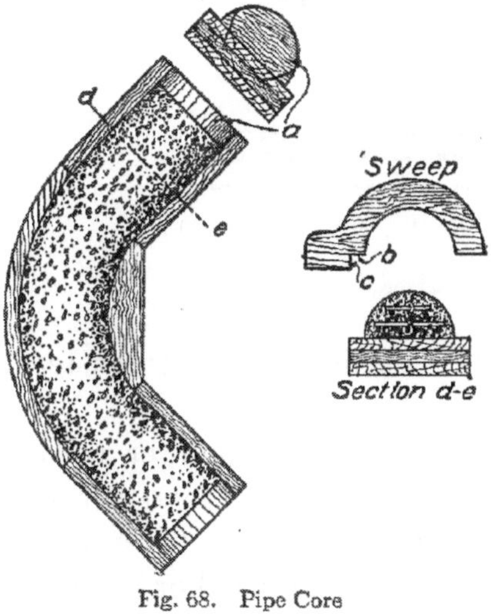

Sweeping. Often, when but one or two large cores are wanted, the cost of making a box is saved by sweeping up the core. This is illustrated in the pipe core shown in Fig. 68.

The pattern-maker gets out 2 core boards and 1 sweep. The boards are made by simply nailing together 3 thicknesses of $\frac{7}{8}$-inch stuff, with the grain of the middle piece crossing that of the others to prevent warping. The outer edges of the boards have the exact curve of the outside of the pipe pattern, and at the ends is tacked a half section of the core, shown at aa. One sweep does for both boards. The curve is cut the exact half section of the core. The edge b equals the

Fig. 68. Pipe Core

thickness of metal in the casting, and the stop *c* acts as a guide along the outer edge of the board.

In making up this core, a thin layer of core sand is spread on the board and the outline of the core swept. On this the rods with their lifting hooks are bedded, and the vent cinders are carefully laid along the middle. The whole general shape is then rammed up in core sand larger than required, and by using the sweep it is brought to exact size. The core is then slicked off, blackened, and baked while still on the board. When both halves are dried, they are pasted together, the same as with smaller work. To

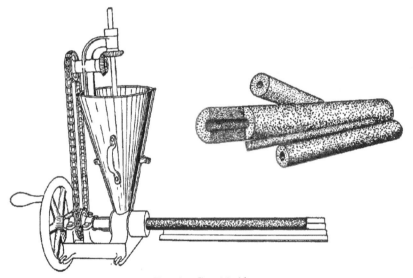

Fig. 69. Core Machine

prevent breaking the lower half when turning it over to paste, it is rolled over on a pile of heap sand.

Core Machines. For making stock cores, round or square, several styles of core machines have been put on the market within the last few years, of which the one illustrated in Fig. 69, is a good representative. This is arranged to be driven by hand or by power. The core sand is placed in the hopper, and by means of a horizontal worm at the bottom it is forced through a nozzle under just the right pressure to pack the core firmly. A clean-cut vent hole is left in the middle of each core. As the core is forced from the nozzle it is received on a corrugated sheet-steel plate, which is moved along to the next groove when the core has run to the full length of the plate.

The advantage of the machine is that with it an apprentice boy can produce a true, smooth, perfectly vented core, in very much less time than could possibly be done by hand-ramming.

Setting Cores

Cylindrical Cores. *Plain Fitting.* Among the following examples showing typical ways of setting and securing cores in molds and of connecting vents, the bolt-hole core, shown at *A*, Fig. 70, illustrates the simplest form of core to set. Only a drag print is necessary; the flat top of the core should just touch the cope surface of the mold. The level may be tested by a straight stick or by

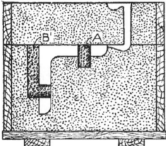

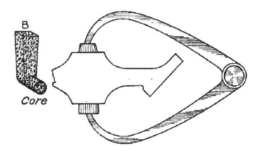

Fig. 70. Bolt-Hole Core   Fig. 71. Calipers

sighting across the joint. If the core is too long, one end may be filed off a little, if too short, a little sand may be filled into the bottom of the print. For longer cores, especially hub cores, a taper print is placed on the cope side of the pattern, and the same taper is given to the end of the core; this guides it to the exact center when the mold is closed. Numerous examples are shown in Pattern-Making. The exact length of the core should be obtained from the pattern with a pair of calipers, as shown in Fig. 71. One point of the calipers should then be placed on the taper end of the core, and the print filled in, or the core shortened in case of variation from the right length. It is well to make a vent hole from the center of each print before setting the core.

With pattern and core boxes properly made, little difficulty should be experienced in setting small horizontal cores for hollow bushings, pipe connections, etc. (See Pattern-Making, Figs. 110,

203, and 210.) The core must fit the print or a poor casting will result. The sand supporting the prints must be tucked firmly enough to withstand the lifting pressure on the core. A scratch

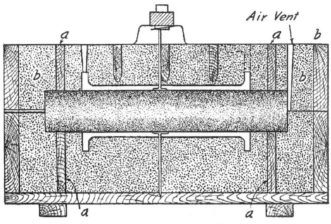

Fig. 72. Supported Body Core

with the point of the trowel along the joint surface from the end of the print to the edge of the flask, will usually take care of the vent.

For larger cores of this character crossbars made to fit snug against the core print are nailed in both drag and cope. See *aaaa*, Fig. 72. These hold the core absolutely firm. The spaces *bb* in the cope, are not packed until the core is set, when it is a simple

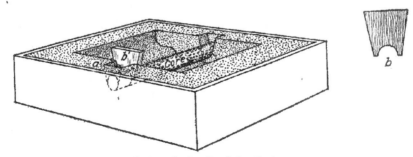

Fig. 73. Setting Core below Surface

matter to ram these spaces and take off an air vent directly from the center of the core.

Holes below Joint Level. There are two methods of coring holes below the level of the joint. One is shown clearly in Fig. 73.

A stock core is set in the bottom of the prints; a wooden template, shown at b and b', is set over the core, and the print a is then packed with molding sand, or *stopped off*, as it is termed.

The other method is shown at B and B', Fig. 70. Here that part of the core which will shape the hole through the casting, is formed on the end of a core which exactly fills the print. A single operation sets the core and stops off the print. For this reason this method is used where a large number of such holes are to be cored.

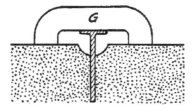

[Fig. 74. Gage for Setting Chaplets.

Setting Chaplets. In setting chaplets, the height of the lower one may be tested with a rule, with a straightedge rested on the prints, or by a gage similar to that shown in Fig. 74. A small boss is usually formed by pressing the trowel handle into the mold where the chaplet is to go.

The cope chaplet is not fastened until the mold is closed, then the stem can be properly wedged down under a bar clamped across the top of the mold.

Projecting Cores. *Balanced Type.* In work where a hole must project well into the casting, but not all the way through it, a balanced core is often used. Such a case is illustrated by the rammer head, Fig. 75. When making this core, let the vent extend through the entire length, then stop up the vent at the small end with a bit of clay after the core is baked.

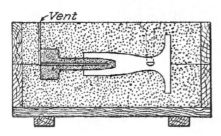

Fig. 75. Small Balanced Core

It is not always practicable to enlarge the print as shown here, but when possible, it reduces the length of print necessary to balance the projecting end and ensures accurate depth to the hole.

Heavy Form. Heavy projecting cores must be supported by chaplets, as illustrated in Fig. 76. Vents may be taken off through a channel and air riser as explained in the section on Venting. Fig. 77 shows the shape of the print on the pattern for this mold at a, the pockets formed by the core are shown at *bb*, and *c* indicates the position of the gate.

Hanging Cores. A core is frequently used to avoid a deep lift for the cope. Suitable wire hangers, shown at *a*, Fig. 78, are bedded in the core when it is made. In setting the core, small annealed wire about No. 20 or

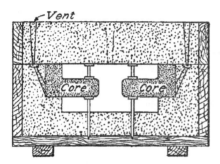

Fig. 76. Large Balanced Core

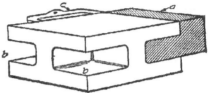

Fig. 77. Shape of Print on Pattern for Projecting Core

No. 24 gage is looped through the hangers, passed through small holes made in the cope, and fastened with a granny twist over an iron bar on top. This bar should bear on the sides of the cope and the core be brought up snug in its print by wedging under its ends. The rigging need only be strong enough to support the weight of the core, for the pressure of metal will force this core firmly into its print with little danger of shifting it. For heavy cores, a lifting eye, as previously illustrated in Fig. 66, takes the place of the wire hanger, and the core is hung by means of a hooked rod with a nut on the end. As shown in Fig. 79, this rod passes through a long washer which bears on a pair of rails, or similar stiff rigging.

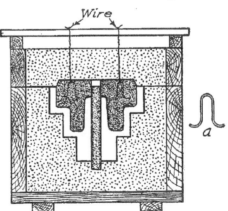

Fig. 79. Section Showing Use of Wire Hangers

Bottom=Anchored Cores. Where possible, the placing of cores in the bottom of molds should be avoided, for in this position, being much lighter than molten iron, they must be secured against a pressure tending to float or lift them. This pressure is proportionate to their depth below the pouring basin. But the metal at the bottom of a mold is cleaner and more sound than that at the top. Therefore, planer beds, large faceplates, and pieces of this character are usually cast face downward, making it necessary to anchor the T-slot cores in the bottom of the mold.

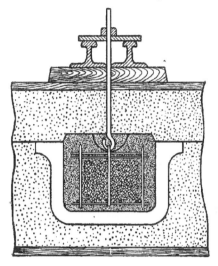

Fig. 79. Section Showing Use of Lifting Eye for Heavy Cores

In some cases, such cores may be held down by driving nails so that their heads project somewhat over the ends of the core, as shown in Fig. 80. If this method is not strong enough, pointed anchors, with a foot on one end, are run through a hole in the core, and are carefully driven into the bottom board, as shown in Fig. 81. Where the work is bedded into the floor, a plank must be set to receive these anchors just below the cinder bed. As in the case of lifting eyes, the holes in the core, into which the foot on the anchor is driven, are smeared with oil and stopped off with green sand.

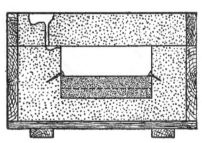

Fig. 80. Section Showing Use of Nails to Hold Cores in Place

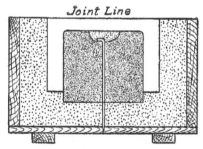

Fig. 81. Section Showing Use of Anchors to Hold Cores in Place

Green-Sand Cores

Expediency in Use. Many times the jobbing foundry may find it expedient, where patterns and core boxes are furnished by the customer, to make certain changes which will reduce the cost of production; for, unhappily, the patterns furnished sometimes show a great desire on the part of the pattern-maker to produce the patterns cheaply, without making due allowance for difficulties encountered in the foundry.

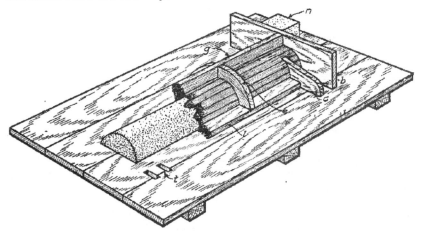

Fig. 82. Half Core with Box Built around It

Typical Instance. The practice of substituting green-sand cores for dry sand has many possibilities. As an example, consider the case of a flange and spigot pipe 72 inches long and 6 inches

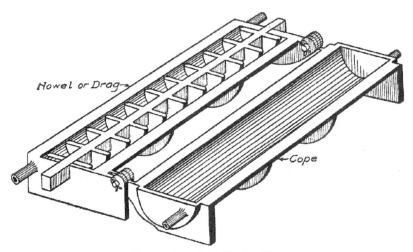

Fig. 83. Completed Mold for Core

inside diameter. The pattern furnished was satisfactory, as was the half-core box, until it was found that the number to be made each day was gradually increasing and the number of half cores

64   FOUNDRY WORK

to be dried was seriously interfering with the production of the regular cores required. It was decided by the foundry management

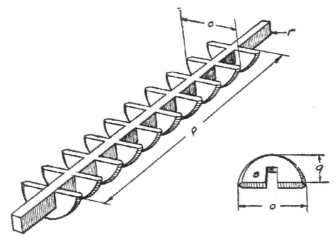

Fig. 84. Cast-Iron Arbor to Carry Core

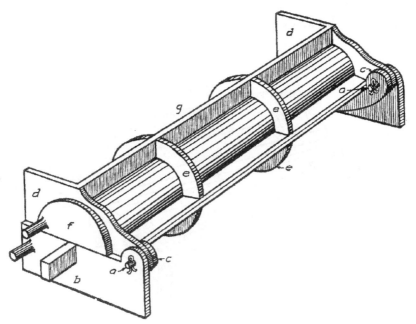

Fig. 85. Mold with Two Halves Together

to adopt the use of a green-sand core, and not only relieve the core ovens, but also effect a considerable saving in core sand and core binders. To make a green-sand core it was necessary to make the core box. The method used was as follows:

First, a half core was made in the original box, and when this

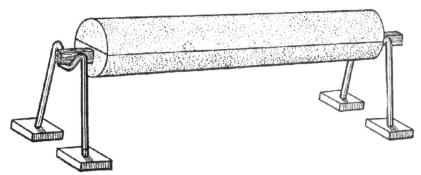

Fig. 86. Complete Core Placed on Horses

was dried it was placed on a new mold board as shown in Fig. 82. Over this was placed lagging of the desired thickness for the casting, as shown in the figure; then over this were placed the loose pieces

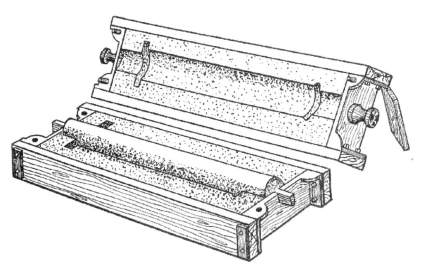

Fig. 87. Complete Mold with Green-Sand Core in Position

b to form the ends of the box and part of the hinge c, also forming a part of hinge on drag half of box, and e and g acting as strengthening ribs.

With these loose pieces in position the drag was duly rammed and rolled over, the cope was rammed and the dry-sand core secured in and lifted off with the cope. The loose pieces were withdrawn from the drag, and the mold was properly finished; when closed and poured, this gave a satisfactory casting of the drag half of the core box. The cope half was made in the same way, the only change being in the shape of the loose pieces forming the ends as seen in Fig. 83.

An arbor being required to carry the green sand, it was made of cast iron, as shown in Fig. 84. To make the green-sand core, first riddle sand in the drag half of the core box; next place the arbor as shown in Fig. 83; then fill and carefully tuck the sand under the flanges on the arbor. The cope is simply filled with sand and rammed, and both drag and cope are struck off level with the joint. The two halves are now closed, as shown in Fig. 85, when the cope may be rolled back to its former position and the core removed from the drag half of the box by lifting an arbor extending through the end of the box.

The core should be placed on horses as shown in Fig. 86, so that it may be repaired if necessary and blackened. Fig. 87 shows the complete mold with green-sand core in position.

In this way a satisfactory core box was made without heavy expense for patterns, as the foundry carpenter or flask man was able to produce the loose pieces from a rough sketch furnished by the foundry foreman.

DUPLICATING CASTINGS

Practical Requisites in Hand Molding. Devising methods for increasing production and decreasing its cost is one of the important problems of modern engineering in the foundry as well as elsewhere. In the jobbing foundry where there is a great variety not only in the patterns themselves, but in the number of castings called for from each pattern, the molder makes up a sand match as already described. On this match he arranges such an assortment of patterns as will fill his flask, and beds them into place. From a well-made sand match two or three hundred molds may be made up. When the desired number of castings is made from one pattern on the match, that one is removed and another one which fits in its place is substituted.

Gated Patterns. For manufacturing purposes thousands of the same casting may be required, calling for more durable patterns and match. Metal patterns are made and as many as can be cast in a flask are soldered to a smoothly finished metal gate pattern. With a draw screw inserted in this gate, all of the patterns may be drawn at once. Two steady pins should be screwed and sweated into the drag side of the gate pattern. These should be of small round brass rod and should project below the deepest point of the patterns, for they guide the pattern as it is being drawn and prevent it from swaying and breaking the edges just as it leaves the sand. Patterns so arranged are termed *gated patterns*.

Permanent Match. When such patterns have a flat joint, a special mold board should be provided, and the patterns stored on the same board. When the joint is irregular, a permanent oil match should be made. Make a strong hardwood frame the size of the flask and about 1 inch deep, with the bottom board arranged to screw on to the back. Nails should be driven into the inner sides hanging parallel to the bottom board. Measure the quantity of sand needed to fill this match.

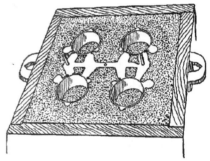

Fig. 88. Oil Match

Mix thoroughly and, while dry, put through a fine sieve one-half this quantity of burnt sand, one-half new molding sand, and about one-fortieth litharge. Temper the same as molding sand, using boiled linseed oil. Ram up the drag and joint the mold very carefully. Put on the match frame and ram up with the above mixture; strike off, and screw on the bottom board. Remove the drag and allow the match to dry for a day with the patterns left in it. A coat of shellac when dry improves the surface. Fig. 88 shows a set of gated patterns bedded in a hard match.

Use of Molding Machines. *Types.* Although there are many styles of molding machines on the market, these may be classified under four general types as follows: stripping-plate machines; squeezers; roll overs; and jar or jolt-ramming machines. The benefits derived from the use of these machines are manifold.

Advantages. If no consideration were taken of the increase in production possible by their use, the improvement in the quality of castings alone would oftentimes warrant their installation, as the decrease in cost of machining castings produced by this method pays good dividends on the investment. The use of unskilled workmen on these machines is no small item in their favor.

Stripping-Plate Machine. The stripping-plate machine is best adapted to that class of work which offers difficulties in drawing the pattern from the sand.

Fig. 89 shows a pattern for a cast gear mounted on the stripping-plate machine. It is obvious that it would require a considerable degree of skill to produce this class of work by the hand-molding method. The pedestal base of the machine has a flat top. The stripping plate is supported above this by a rigid open framework. Working in guides carried on the sides of this framework is the drawing frame, made to rise or descend by a strong crank and connecting rod. On top of this drawing frame and parallel to the stripping plate is screwed the plate to which the pattern is fastened. The stripping plate is cast with an opening which leaves about 1 inch clear all around the pattern. When both pattern and stripping plate are properly set in place, this space is filled with babbitt metal, this being an easy way to secure a nice fit.

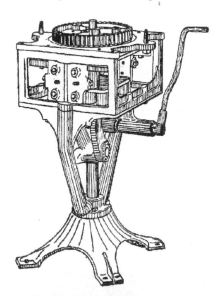

Fig. 89. Typical Molding Machine

In many cases there may be an interior body of sand to be supported when the pattern is drawn. To accomplish this stools are used. A leg screwed into the stool plate supports the stool at the exact level of the stripping plate. The stool plate is fastened to the flat top of the machine inside of the box-like framework which supports the stripping plate, as seen in Fig. 90.

A flask is inverted on the machine, rammed, vented, and struck off. Movement of the crank lever at the side draws the pattern;

and the mold then is removed and set on a level sand floor, thus doing away with bottom boards. A second stripping plate and pattern is used for ramming the cope boxes.

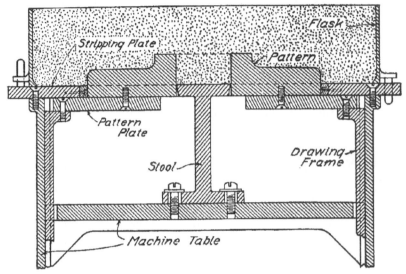

Fig. 90. Molding Stool with Pattern in Place

Pulleys are manufactured on molding machines of this type, as shown by the equipment illustrated in Fig. 91. The rim patterns

Fig. 91. Pulley Molding Machine

have the form of long hollow cylinders and can readily be set for any desired width of face. The hub carrying the core print separates from the spokes, lifts off in the mold, and is drawn by hand. The arm patterns are so flat and smoothly rounded that the mold is

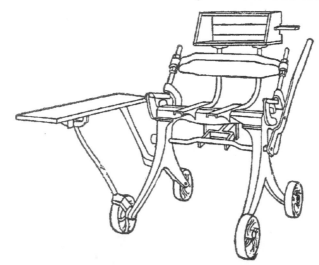

Fig. 92. Simple Molding Machine or Squeezer

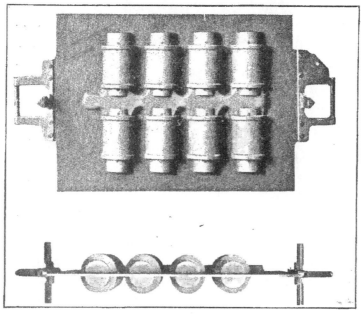

Fig. 93. Match Plate
Courtesy of Tabor Manufacturing Company, Philadelphia, Pennsylvania

easily lifted off of them with little fear of breaking the sand. The cope and drag molds are both alike for a pulley mold.

Squeezer. Fig. 92 shows a type of machine known as the hand squeezer, which only packs the sand. Here the patterns are carried on two sides of a plate set between the cope and drag, as in Fig. 93. Both boxes are filled with sifted sand and set on the machine. The boards are made to follow inside of the flask. The molder's weight on the lever compresses the sand.

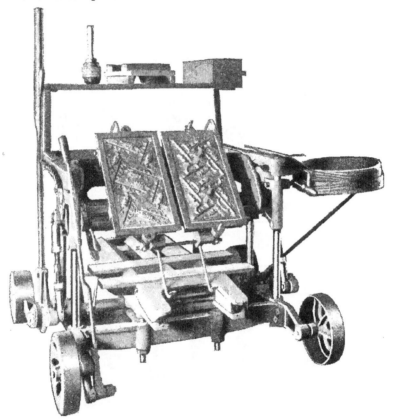

Fig. 94. Hand Squeezing Machine with Cope and Drag Patterns Attached to Portable Table
Courtesy of Arcade Manufacturing Company, Freeport, Illinois

The sprue is cut by a thin hollow steel tube called a sprue-cutter, which is pressed through the cope sand by the molder before separating the flask. In separating the mold the cope is first lifted from the drag, and the plate is gently rapped and lifted from the drag. To make a clean lift when parts of the patterns project in the cope, a second molder raps with an iron bar between the battens of the bottom board while the cope is being drawn off.

72   FOUNDRY WORK

Such machines are used chiefly on thin work which vents and solidifies very rapidly—for the outer surfaces of the drag and cope are apt to be rammed so hard that they might choke the vent on heavier castings.

A somewhat different style of hand squeezer is shown in Fig. 94, which shows both cope and drag pattern plates attached to a portable

Fig. 95. Beginning the Operation with Hand Molding Machine. Two Halves of Flask in Position
Courtesy of Arcade Manufacturing Company, Freeport, Illinois

table. Beginning the operation, the table holding the plates is turned face up with the two halves of the flask in position as shown in Fig. 95. After the sand is thrown in the flask and the surplus scraped off, the bottom boards are placed in position and held by four clamps. Next, the table is rolled over as in Fig. 96. The ramming or squeezing operation is accomplished by pulling down the long lever at the left of the machine, as shown in Fig. 97. At this point the clamps holding the cope and the bottom are automatically released.

Fig. 98 illustrates the method of drawing the patterns. The lever is slowly lifted with the left hand, while the operator raps the vibrating pin with a mallet held in the right hand. When the long

Fig. 96. Table Rolled Over Preparatory to Squeezing
Courtesy of Arcade Manufacturing Company, Freeport, Illinois

lever is returned to its upright position, the two halves of the mold rest on the sliding platform. This is drawn forward in the position shown in Fig. 99. The mold is then closed, the flask removed, and the completed mold carried to its position on the floor for pouring. Snap flasks are best adapted for this style of machine.

Roll Over. The roll-over machine which is illustrated by Fig. 100, has the pattern mounted on a wooden match plate as shown at *A*,

74   FOUNDRY WORK

which when in position to receive flask is resting on pins at BB. The mold is rammed by hand in the usual manner, the bottom board being clamped on by a special device to the frame C. The mold is next rolled over and rests at A. The pattern is withdrawn by the use of the foot pedal E, the operator meantime rapping the match plate

Fig. 97. Ramming or Squeezing Operation
Courtesy of Arcade Manufacturing Company, Freeport, Illinois

with a wooden maul. This type of machine is best adapted to side floor work, the grate bar here shown being a good sample.

Power Operation. The above-mentioned types show only hand machines which have been in general use for a considerable period of time, but the last decade has shown a wonderful change in this branch of foundry practice; indeed so great is the advance that hardly a month passes that there does not appear some new featuer. The most important advancement, of course, was the adaptation of power, usually compressed air being resorted to, but more recently there has been quite a tendency to utilize electricity.

Power Squeezer. Fig. 101 shows compressed air applied to the squeezer type of molding machine. This machine is designed

Fig. 98. Drawing the Patterns. Use of Mallet
Courtesy of Arcade Manufacturing Company, Freeport, Illinois

especially for use in molding light snap-flask work in large or small quantities, and the method of pattern fitting depends upon the number of castings to be made from one pattern.

A careful study of the line drawing of this machine shown in Fig. 102 should give a clear understanding of the working parts of the power squeezer, the numbered ones being identified as follows:

76　FOUNDRY WORK

Fig. 99. Two Halves of Mold in Open Position
Courtesy of Arcade Manufacturing Company, Freeport, Illinois

1. Yoke
2. Left-hand stop for yoke
3. Yoke handle
4. Pressure gage
5. ¼-inch air cock
6. Eye bolt
7. Left-hand strain bar
8. Right-hand strain bar
9. Right-hand yoke stop
10. Platen
11. Knee-pad rod
12. Air hose from knee valve to vibrator
13. Air hose from knee valve to supply
14. Hose guard
15. Knee pad
16. Knee starting valve
17. Cylinder base
18. Piston
19. Piston ring
20. Counterbalance spring
21. Adjustment block for spring seat
22. Adjustment-block set screw
23. Trunnion
24. Bracket for lower spring seat
25. No. 5 snap oiler
26. Trunnion shaft
27. Pop throttle-valve lever
28. Valve-lever stud
29. Throttle-stop segment
30. Valve sand guard
31. Valve spring for exhaust
32. Adjustable strain-bar stop
33. Valve body
34. L hose nipple
35. Straight hose nipple
36. Valve bracket
37. Taper pins, trunnion to shaft
38. Blow valve
39. Blow-valve hose

Attention is called to the fact that the production of the power squeezer exceeds that of the hand squeezer by 15 to 30 per cent. For description of various ways of mounting patterns, see Pattern-Making.

Power Roll-Over. A power roll-over power-draft machine is shown in Fig. 103. This is designed to handle side floor work,

Fig. 100. Roll-Over Molding Machine with Pattern Withdrawn
Courtesy of Tabor Manufacturing Company, Philadelphia, Pennsylvania

and has a straight draft of 8 inches and sufficient power to roll over a weight of 1000 pounds. It will be noted that as in the hand roll-over the patterns are mounted on wooden match plates, the small expense of which makes this style of machine very effective in jobbing shops where but few castings are made from a pattern at a time.

In Fig. 104 is shown the latest type of this machine with the flask shown in position ready for bar ramming. Fig. 105 shows the

78 FOUNDRY WORK

mold partly rolled over; the mold rolled over and partly withdrawn is shown in Fig. 106. The view given in Fig. 107 shows the finished mold on one side and the pattern back in place.

The working parts of the above machine are shown in Fig. 108, and are as follows:

1. Roll-over frame
2. Air cylinder
3. Link
4. Wedge leveling device
5. Adjustable support for leveling device
6. Operating valve and lever
7. Vibrator

The plunger is made hollow and acts as an oil tank into which air under pressure is admitted when the machine is to be operated. When air pressure is admitted to the plunger, the oil is forced through

Fig. 101. 10-Inch Squeezer Operated by Compressed Air
Courtesy of Tabor Manufacturing Company, Philadelphia, Pennsylvania

a port into the cylinder, causing the plunger to rise and by means of its link connections to roll over the mold which is deposited on the leveling device. After the flask has been unclamped air is again admitted to the plunger, causing the pattern to be drawn vertically the full draft of the machine, at which point the link

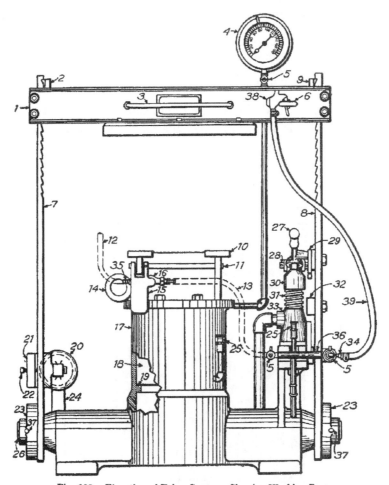

Fig. 102. Elevation of Tabor Squeezer Showing Working Parts

connections cause the roll-over frame to return to its initial position ready to receive another flask.

Jolt-Ramming Machine. The jar or jolt-ramming machine is used for all classes of work from light work up to the largest floor work made in green sand, the limit being only the capacity of the machine itself, which varies from a few hundred pounds to many thousands of pounds. Large engine beds are a good example of the castings produced on the heavy-duty machines.

Fig. 103. Power Roll-Over, Power Draft Molding Machine with 12-Inch Straight Draft
Courtesy of Tabor Manufacturing Company, Philadelphia, Pennsylvania

Fig. 104. Latest Type of Tabor Molding Machine with Flask Ready for Ramming

Patterns mounted on heavy wooden match plates are used in the manner hereafter described. The flask is first placed on the drag half of the pattern board, and the flask filled with sand. By the use of an upset, usually about 4 inches deep, it is possible to heap sufficient sand on the flask to insure its being filled after the ramming has taken place. The flask must be securely clamped to the pattern plate, when both may be listed by the traveling crane and placed on the table of the jarring machine, which in the heavy-duty machines is on the foundry-floor level; the working parts of the machine being below and resting on a rigid concrete foundation. Here, air under

Fig. 105. Machine with Mold Partly Rolled Over
Courtesy of Tabor Manufacturing Company, Philadelphia, Pennsylvania

pressure is allowed to enter the cylinder, and, acting on the plunger, which in turn lifts the table usually about 4 inches, when the air is suddenly exhausted, allows the table to drop heavily on the anvil. The number of blows required to pack the sand must be determined by experience. The time required to ram the largest mold is but a small fraction of that consumed by hand-ramming.

Fig. 109 is an illustration of one of the simplest styles of this type of machine. Fig. 110 shows the working parts of the same machine.

Fig. 106. Mold Completely Rolled Over and Partly Withdrawn
Courtesy of Tabor Manufacturing Company, Philadelphia, Pennsylvania

Fig. 107. Finished Mold on One Side and Pattern in Place
Courtesy of Tabor Manufacturing Company, Philadelphia, Pennsylvania

FOUNDRY WORK 83

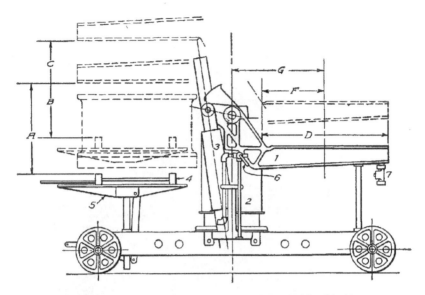

Fig. 108. Diagram of Working Parts of the Tabor Molding Machine

Fig. 109. Simple Type of Jolt-Ramming Machine
Courtesy of American Molding Machine Company, Terre Haute, Indiana

A quite distinct style of jolt machine, called an electropneumatic jolt-ramming machine, is shown in Fig. 111, the unique feature being the motor-driven compressor without a clutch, spring, cam,

84 FOUNDRY WORK

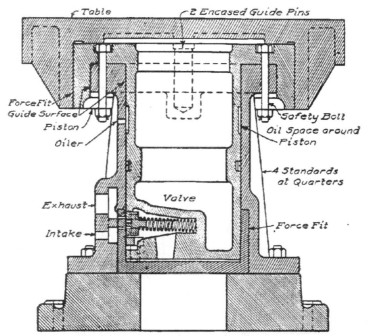

Fig. 110. Section of American Jolt-Ramming Machine

Fig. 111. Krause Electropneumatic Jolt Rammer
Courtesy of Vulcan Engineering Sales Company, Chicago, Illinois

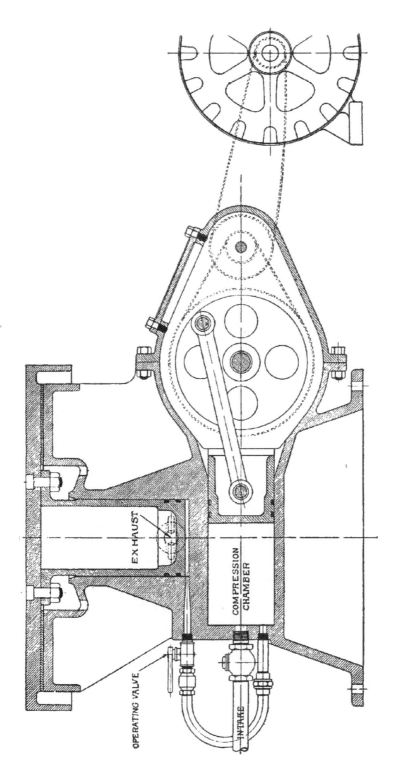

Fig. 112. Section of Krause Jolt Rammer Showing Transmission and Unique Compressor

or valve. A very little study of Fig. 112 should make clear its radical features.

Automatic Squeezer. Fig. 113 illustrates an automatic molding machine of the squeezer type. The operator places the flask and bottom board in position, then by simply pressing on the starting lever the filling of the flask with sand, the ramming and the drawing of the pattern is completely automatic and accomplished in about

Fig. 113. Automatic Molding Machine of the Squeezer Type
Courtesy of Berkshire Manufacturing Company, Cleveland, Ohio

eight seconds or some six or seven hundred molds per day. This machine is best adapted to the production of small duplicate work such as small pipe fittings.

Roller-Ramming Machine. The very distinctive type of molding machine shown in Fig. 114 is known as the roller-ramming machine. It is best adapted to long work of comparatively thin cross-section, of which a cornice section would be a good example. This class of work could not be produced readily on any of the previously mentioned types of machines. Fig. 115 is a detailed drawing of Fig. 114.

Fig. 114. Moldar Roller-Ramming Machine in Operation
Courtesy of Richey, Browne and Donald, Maspeth, New York

The success of any and all molding machines depends on the intelligent selection of the type best suited for the work in hand.

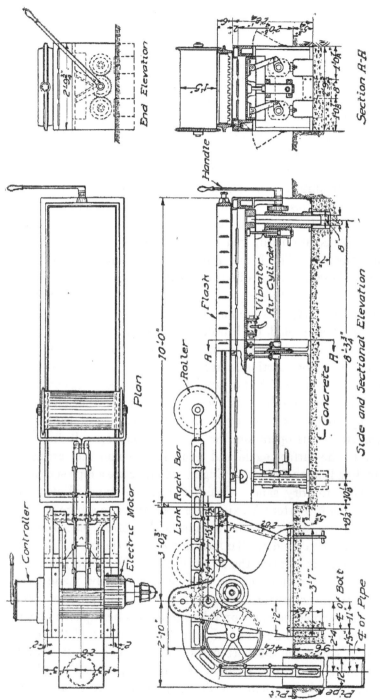

Fig. 115. Plan and Elevation of Mortar Roller-Ramming Machine

FOUNDRY WORK

DRY=SAND WORK

Characteristic Features. This branch of molding becomes a separate trade in shops where the work is done continually. The dry-sand molder must use the same precautions as the green-sand molder in setting gates and risers, and in fastening his sand with crossbars and gaggers. At the same time, he works with a core-sand mixture next his patterns and backs this with a coarse molding sand, so that he must combine the skill and judgment of both the green-sand molder and the core maker. The venting of dry-sand work must be ample, as in the case of cores, but it is simpler than in core work, because the core mixture surrounds the casting so that vents may be taken off in all directions.

Iron flasks are used, generally provided with trunnions to facilitate turning. The facing mixture is the same as that used for making large cores, as discussed in the section on Core Work; the remainder of the flask is packed with the same sand after it has been used. The patterns are made and used the same as with green sand, only they should be brushed over with linseed, crude-oil, or other heavy oil, before ramming. In some shops oil is brushed over the joint before parting sand is thrown on. After the pattern is drawn, the mold is finished by applying a heavy coat of good black wash. When the sand has absorbed the moisture so that all glisten has disappeared, this blacking is slicked over. Great care must be exercised in this operation, for too much slicking will draw the moisture to the surface again and result in scabs on the casting.

Molding Engine Cylinder. Engine cylinders are a representative line of work for dry sand. Consider a simple type of cylinder, such as shown in Pattern-Making, Fig. 244, to have a bore of from 16 to 26 inches, and with the exhaust-outlet flange placed above the center of the cylinder. To facilitate setting the cores, the pattern may be split through the steam chest. The flange just mentioned should be molded in the drag, and should be made loose and draw in the opposite direction from the main pattern. The cylinder core should be made on a barrel, as will be explained later, and the mold poured on end to insure sound metal and to reduce the casting strain on the port cores. The flask is made with a round opening in one end to allow the core to project through it. This opening is larger than the diameter of the core to allow for gates and risers. There must be another opening at the side of the flask adjacent to the steam-chest core to provide for fastening these cores. Iron plates serve for flask boards and there should be a hole in the drag plate in line with the exhaust core to allow for venting and fastening its end.

One-half of Fig. 116 shows the end view of the flask. The other half shows a section through the middle of the completed mold. Here A is the hollow cylinder core, B is the chest core, C the live-steam core hung in the cope, and D the exhaust core. The flask is packed in a manner similar to green sand.

Use of Cover-Core. The method of molding the exhaust flange, however, has not previously been explained. To do this,

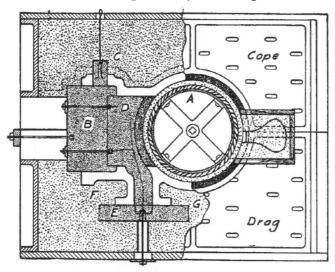

Fig. 116. Molding a Cylinder

proceed packing the drag until the pattern is covered. Tuck the facing carefully underneath the flange, setting in rods as in core work, to strengthen the overhanging portions. Make a flat joint, FG at the level of the top of the flange, then carefully fit over the print of the flange the cover-core E, and fix its position with nails driven into the joint at its corners. Now remove the cover-core, draw the flange, and finish that part of the mold with black wash and slicking. When this is accomplished, replace the cover-core, place a short piece of pipe over its central vent, and finish ramming the drag. This method may be used in many cases, both in dry-sand

FOUNDRY WORK

and in green-sand work where a small detail of the casting requires a separate joint surface.

A sectional plan looking down on the drag is shown in Fig. 117. When the mold has been properly finished and baked, the drag is brought from the oven and set on a pair of stout horses. The cylinder core is first set in place, then the exhaust core is set in its

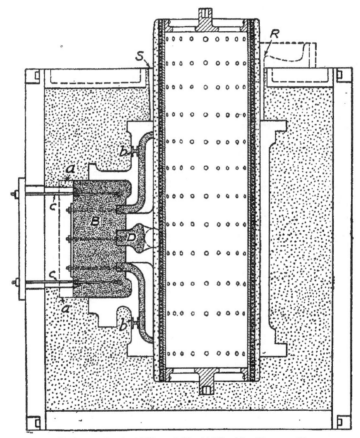

Fig. 117. Sectional Plan of Fig. 116 Looking Down on Drag

drag print and held close to the cylinder core, while the port and chest cores, previously pasted and fastened, are lowered into the chest print. The chest print is cut a little long at *aa*, to allow its core to be drawn back slightly, while the exhaust core is entered into its place between the port cores. Then all of the cores are set forward into position, the chaplets *bb* set, the space *aa* tightly packed again, and the anchor bolts *cc* placed in position and made fast.

The drag print of the exhaust core is made fast from underneath the drag plate. When all the cores have been firmly fastened, the cope is closed on, and the two boxes clamped at the flanges and set up on end. The runner R and the riser S were cut and finished before baking, the basins must be built in green sand after the mold is closed.

Making Barrel Core. Loam is used here for the outer shell of the core. It is probably the simplest job in which a loam mixture is employed, and is made by a core maker more frequently than by the higher paid loam molder. Barrel cores are used where the core is long and can best be supported at the ends only; for example, in gas and water pipes and cylinder work.

Loam. Loam is a facing mixture, of the consistency of mortar, applied to the face of the core or mold. It contains fire sand with a bond of strong porous molding sand moistened with a thick clay wash. A small proportion of organic matter in the shape of horse manure is put in to aid the bond and to leave the crust of loam more fragile by burning out as the casting cools. Proportions of the mixture will vary according to locality, but the principles already cited hold here as with other molding compounds. With too much bond the loam works easier but tends to choke the vents when casting. With not enough it is weak and is liable to break, cut, or crumble under strain. A typical mixture is as follows

Loam Mixtures

Material	Mixed by Hand (parts)	Mixed by Mill (parts)
Fire sand	10	10
Strong coarse molding sand	4	3
Horse manure	$1\frac{1}{2}$	2
Temper	Thick clay wash	Thick clay wash

The advantages of loam cores are that they are lighter, cheaper to make, and carry off the gases faster than do dry-sand cores.

Method. The method is as follows: A piece of pipe about 3 inches smaller than the outside diameter of the core is selected to form the center. The pipe is perforated with a large number of holes. If the pipe is more than 3 or 4 inches in diameter, centers or trunnions are riveted in the ends to serve as bearings. The pipe is arranged to revolve freely on a pair of iron horses, as shown in Fig. 118. A crank handle is attached by which the pipe may be turned. A couple of wraps of hay rope are first given around one end of the pipe, and the loose end is pinned flat by a nail run under these strands. Tight wrapping is then continued to the other end of the pipe, where the rope is fastened in a similar manner and cut off. Hay rope should be made of long wisps tightly twisted. Sizes vary from $\frac{3}{4}$ to 1 inch. Where only a small amount of hay rope is used, it is bought ready made. Foundries using large quantities

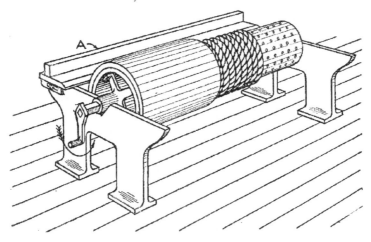

Fig. 118. Making Loam Core for Cylinder

are equipped with one or more machines built especially for making this rope.

The first coat of loam is rubbed on with the hands, then well pressed in with the flat side of a board as the barrel is slowly revolved. When this has set, the core board A is placed in position, and the roughing coat worked on to the core to within about $\frac{1}{4}$ inch of finished size. The core is now dried in the oven. Placing the core again on the standards, the finishing coat of slip is applied with the core board while the core is still hot. The diameter is tested with calipers and brought to required size by slight adjustment of the sweep board A. When the core has been built to size, move the loam back from the edge of the board A, then withdraw the board while the barrel is still in motion.

Slip. Slip or skinning loam is made by thinning regular loam as it is rubbed through a No 8 sieve. The heat of the core is usually sufficient to dry this slip coat enough so that black wash may be brushed on and slicked, as in dry-sand work, before running the core into the oven again for its final baking.

The service of the hay rope on a barrel core is twofold: it furnishes a surface over the smooth metal of the barrel to which loam will adhere; and it is elastic enough to give as the casting shrinks around the core. The hay slowly burns out after the casting has set, and this frees the barrel so that it can easily be withdrawn and used again.

LOAM MOLDING

Skill Required. The loam molder requires the greatest all-around skill in the whole range of foundry work. He must know all the tricks of the core room and dry-sand shop, and most of those in green sand. Added to all this he must have a practical working knowledge of the principles of drawing and must possess to a large degree the foresight of the designer.

In order to save time and lumber in the pattern shop, only a set of sweeps is provided if the mold is simple, and these, with blue prints of the piece wanted, are all the molder has to work from. In intricate work, such as a modern Corliss cylinder, a skeleton pattern carrying the steam chests, etc , in accurate position is made, and in some very crooked work a pattern is furnished complete. As a rule, however, the loam molder must rely upon his own skill and ingenuity for the best method of constructing each detail of the work.

Rigging. The equipment for the loam floor varies in different shops. In Fig. 119 are shown the essential features of an equipment for sweeping-up circular forms.

Spindle. The spindle a should be large enough not to spring when being used, and long enough to conveniently clear the highest mold. A piece of 2-inch shafting is a handy size, for with it the sweeps may be made uniformly 1 inch less than the required diameter and placed snug to the spindle when set up, and the correct size of mold is ensured. This spindle should revolve smoothly in a step b. The step shown may be set at any convenient place on the floor. It has a long taper bearing, as shown in section A, capable of holding a 5-foot spindle without need of any top bearing. The three arms serve to

FOUNDRY WORK 95

make the step set firmly, and upon them any plate may be readily leveled up. Where a tall spindle is used, the spindle socket is more shallow; the step may be cast without arms and be bedded in the floor. The top of the spindle is steadied by the bracket c. This must carry a bearing box so designed that the spindle may be readily set in position or removed. And the bracket must swing back out of the way when any parts of the mold are to be handled by the crane.

Sweeps. The sweeps are attached by means of the sweep arm d. The detail B shows one method of clamping the sweep arm to the spindle by using a key. The arm is offset so that one face hangs in

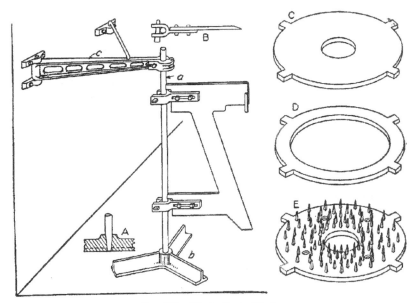

Fig. 119. Rig for Loam Work

line with the center of the spindle. Bolting the face side of the sweep to this brings the working edge in a true radial plane. Sweeps are usually made from pine about $1\frac{1}{8}$ inches thick. The working edge is cut to the exact contour of the form to be swept, and then is beveled so that the edge actually sweeping the surface is only about $\frac{3}{8}$ inch. For very accurate work or when sweeps are to be much used, the edge is faced with thin strap iron to prevent wear.

Plates. We have seen that the walls of green- and dry-sand molds are supported by sand packed into flasks and that these flasks may be lifted, turned up sideways, or rolled completely over to suit the convenience of the workman. The facing which forms the wall of a loam mold is supported by brickwork built upon flat plates of cast iron, and laid in a weak mortar of mud. From the nature of their construction, therefore, these molds must always be kept perpendicular when being handled. The parts may be raised, lowered, or moved in any direction horizontally, but they must not be tipped or rolled over.

The plates are cast in open sand molds, as illustrated in Fig. 56. Two methods are employed to provide for handling them by the crane;

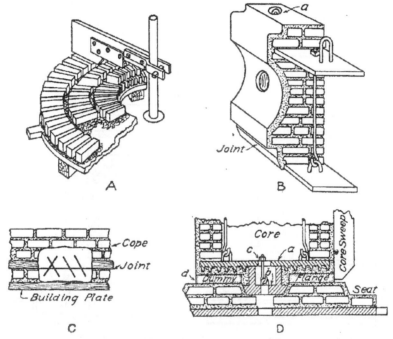

Fig. 120. Laying-Up Loam Work

either lugs are cast on the edges of the plates, as in *C*, *D*, and *E*, Fig. 119, or wrought staples are cast in the plates, as shown in *B*, Fig. 120, or in the crown plate of the main cylinder core, Fig. 123.

Three typical plates for a loam job are shown in Fig. 119. *C* is the building plate; it should be at least 18 or 20 inches larger than the largest diameter of the casting to be made, and thick enough to support the weight of the entire mold without springing. *D* shows a cope ring; its inside diameter should clear the casting 2 inches on all sides. The face should be 8 to 12 inches wide, depending upon the height of the mold. E shows a cover plate; its diameter equals the outside diameter of the brickwork on that part of the mold which it covers. Here the loam facing is placed directly on the iron, and must be supported when the plate stands vertically or is turned completely over as in C, Fig. 122. To hold the loam in this way, fingers or stickers are cast on these plates. This is accomplished by simply printing the end of a tapered stick into the bed of the open mold which

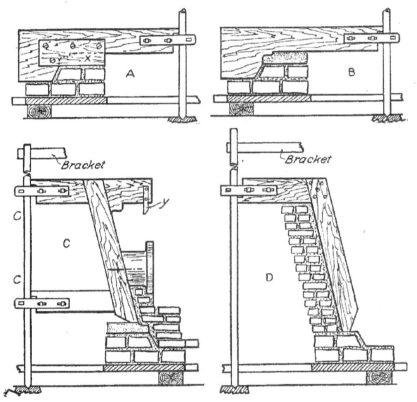

Fig. 121. Steps in Sweeping Up Type Mold

shapes the plates. These sticker plates are often used for a purpose similar to the core E, Fig. 116, and shape the outer face of a picked-out flange. This is illustrated in D, Fig. 122.

Materials. *Brick.* Common red brick is best for making loam molds, Figs. 120 to 123. It should be free from glaze and have a uniform texture, so that the pieces will break clean when it is necessary to fit them to the shape. An old 12-inch half-round file makes a handy tool for cutting these. Sometimes brick is molded up from loam, and air-dried. It is much more fragile than red brick, and may be used in pockets, or where the shell of the casting is quite thin, and ordinary brick might resist the shrinkage strain to such an extent as to endanger cracking the casting.

Mud. For laying up the brickwork, mud is used, loam facing being applied only to those surfaces which come in actual contact

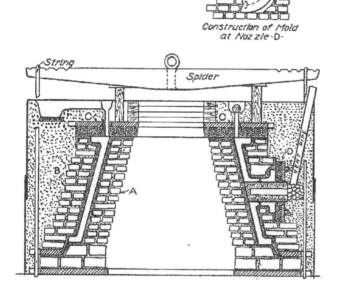

Fig. 122. Complete Typical Loam Mold

with the iron. Mud is made from burnt loam or old floor sand, mixed with clay wash to the consistency of mortar.

Facing. The composition of loam facing and slip have already been given under the description of making a barrel core.

Cinders. Cinders are an important material in this work. Their size will depend upon their position in the mold. For working in between brick, the cinders should be crushed if necessary, put through a No. 4 sieve to remove smallest pieces, then passed through a No. 2 sieve to remove the larger pieces.

FOUNDRY WORK 99

Principles of Work. *Parts of Mold.* The names of the main parts of a loam mold differ somewhat from those applied when molding in flasks. As will be seen from the section, Fig. 122, there are three main divisions in the mold: A, which corresponds to the drag in a three-part mold, is called the *core*. B, which corresponds to the cheek, is called the *cope* in loam work. And C, which serves the same purpose as the cope of a green-sand mold, is spoken of as the *cover* in loam molding. When the central core is actually made a separate piece, as in Fig. 123, the lower part of the mold is called the *bed* or *foundation*.

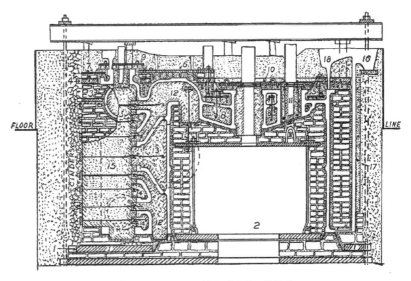

Fig. 123. Loam Mold for Marine Cylinder

Laying-Up. In laying-up a loam mold, Fig. 120, set the plate central with the spindle and approximately level. Then set the sweep and finish leveling the plate until repeated measurements at the four quarters of the circle show a uniform space between the lower edge of the sweep and the surface of the plate. For the building plate this measurement should be 5 inches; for a sticker plate the sweep should clear the sticker points by $\frac{1}{2}$ to 1 inch according to the thickness of the casting.

The hands are used in spreading mud or loam upon the plates or brickwork when building the mold. The brick must always be set well apart, leaving a space at least the width of a finger between them. Fill in these spaces with fine cinders. The reason for this is fourfold. It facilitates drying; it provides good vent; it gives or crushes sufficiently when the casting shrinks not to cause undue strain; and it reduces the labor in cleaning. In each course of brick the joints should lead as directly as possible away from the casting, but the joints should be broken between courses. These points are illustrated in the sketch A, Fig. 120. As shown, the first two courses of the core are usually set edgewise. For the rest of the core and for the cope, the bricks are laid flat. These bricks run lengthwise around the circumference, with a course of headers about every four to six courses.

Venting. Cinders between brick form the ordinary means of leading the vent from the loam facing. In confined places or pockets, as, for example, between the flange D and the main casting, Fig. 122, additional provision is made by laying long wisps of straw between the courses of brick. The service of the straw is similar to that of the hay rope of a barrel core.

Jointing. The joint in loam work is made by a plate lifting away from a loam seat, or by two loam surfaces separating one from another. In forming the first of these the loam seat is swept up and allowed to partially set, then the surface is brushed with oil, and parting sand is thrown over it. The seat should then be soft enough to allow the iron plate to sink into it sufficiently to find a good bearing, while the oil and parting sand will prevent the loam facing from adhering to the underside of the plate. For the loam-to-loam joint, the same method is used, but the loam is allowed to set somewhat harder before building the joint against it. The angle of the main joint should be about 1 in 4 inches.

To insure the different parts being put together for casting in exactly the same position in which they were built, a guide surface of loam is smoothed across the joint at three or four convenient points on the outside walls of the mold. These surfaces are each marked differently with the edge of the trowel, similar to the cut at C, Fig. 120.

Drawback. To properly separate and finish some molds, it is necessary to lift away a portion of the mold before lifting the main part. Such a portion is called a *drawback*. The drawback is always built up in position against a pattern or sweep. With the cover plate, which on a smaller scale often serves the same purpose, as at

D, Fig. 122, a flat joint is made on the outer wall of the mold, but the cover plate is swept up separately. At 3, Fig. 123, is shown a drawback which carries but a few courses of brick. It may be lifted away by lugs cast in the drawback plate with little danger of displacing its brickwork in handling.

If the shape of the drawback renders it impracticable to handle it by the lower plate alone, the brickwork should be bound together by means of hook bolts which clamp on a top plate set sufficiently below the upper joint to be entirely protected from the metal. This upper plate has staples cast in it by which the whole drawback may be lifted. At B, Fig. 120, the typical construction of such a piece is illustrated. The drawing shows one-half the length of the brickwork removed to bring out more clearly the rigging used. The upper end of the second lifting staple shows at a, with the loam cut neatly away to allow hooking into the staple.

Where the main core lifts away or is to be covered with metal over its top, it must be bound together in a similar manner. This is illustrated in the mold for the marine-engine cylinder, Fig. 123, in which both of these conditions occur.

Example of Internal Flange. If a casting has an internal flange requiring thickness of metal underneath the main core, the rigging will be altered to fit these conditions, as shown at D, Fig. 120. In this sketch a is a sticker plate and so will carry the loam necessary to face the bottom of the core. To this the small bearing plate b is securely bolted by the hook bolt c. This plate must set directly upon solid brickwork, as it carries the weight of the entire core. On this bearing plate are cast three studs which firmly support the sticker plate at the required height above the flange surface. The sticker plate carrying this print is filled with loam or dry sand and given a first baking, then swept to a finished surface before being inverted into position. Then the remainder of the core is built up on top and bound together, as in the previous example. Another way to form the bottom of this core is to sweep up a dummy flange d, in mud. Set the bearing plate b, and work the loam in around the studs to form the short neck to the level of the top of the flange. Then spread over this flange $\frac{1}{2}$ inch of loam and bed down onto this the sticker plate which has been previously filled with loam and dried, as is described below. Be sure that the studs on b bring up to a firm bearing against the plate a, then clamp tight with hook bolts and proceed to sweep-up the body of the core.

Bedding Cover Plate. In case a cover plate must be bedded down against a flat surface, as in the example just mentioned, or must take the impression of an irregular surface on the top of a mold or pattern, as illustrated in Fig. 123, the method to pursue is as follows: After casting, invert the plate and carefully lower it into position, and make sure that all fingers clear the surface by at least $\frac{1}{2}$ or $\frac{3}{4}$ inch. Now set the plate with the fingers up, fill in with loam enough to just clear their tops, leaving the proper openings for runners, risers, tie bolts, etc., and dry thoroughly in the oven. Upon removal from the oven, invert and try this loam cover again on the surface it must fit; scrape away any portions which project too much. Now hoist away the cover and coat the face with clay wash. Having previously prepared the surface of the pattern with oil and any loam joint with oil and parting sand, spread an even thickness of fresh loam all over and bed the plate down upon this. The cover plate, being still hot, will, by the aid of the clay wash, cause the thin layer of fresh loam to dry out and stick fast to the dry loam forming the body of the plate.

Simple Mold. As an example of a simple loam mold let us consider the details of a large casting, having the shape of the frustrum of a cone, with a flange at the top and bottom and a flanged nozzle projecting from one side, such as the section clearly shown in Fig. 122.

Foundation. Set the sweep, level up the building plate, and, building the brickwork as shown in A, Fig. 120, sweep the seat, joint, and bottom surface of flange, as shown at A, Fig. 121. The lower flange may be formed by a wooden pattern furnished by the pattern maker, but it is more common to have the sweep made with the small board x, which may be removed. By doing this the exact shape of the flange may be swept up without changing the main sweep, as shown at B, Fig. 121. This dummy flange, as it is called, is swept-up from fairly stiff mud.

Cope. The next step is to seat the cope ring and set the cope sweep, as shown at C, Fig. 121. This sweep shapes the mold for the outside of the casting, for the top flange, and for the top joint of the mold. Loam is thrown, a handful at a time, against the joint and dummy flange, and the engaging faces of bricks are rubbed with loam and pressed into position.

When the top of the lower flange is reached in this way, the courses are laid-up for about 2 feet before the loam is spread upon their inner surface and struck off. This method is pursued until the mold is built to its full height.

The projecting nozzle is formed by a wooden pattern; this should be well oiled, and the brickwork and loam laid-up under it to support it at the proper level, as given by the center line on the pattern and corresponding line on the sweep. Such projections frequently must be supported in their exact position with reference to the main pattern by temporary wooden framework or skeleton work until the mold is built up under them.

A finger y nailed to the top member of the cope sweep, shapes the guide surfaces on the outside of the mold which are used to center the cover plate in closing the mold. A similar finger exactly the same distance from the spindle, is fastened to the sweep used to form the cover plate.

After the finishing coat of slip has been swept on the surface of the cope, a joint surface about 4 inches wide is struck off flush with the outer face of the nozzle and that pattern is drawn out.

Then the whole cope is lifted off and set on iron supports where it may be conveniently finished with black wash and slicks. It is then baked over night in the oven.

Center Core. The dummy flange is now entirely removed from the first part swept, the core sweep is set, D, Fig. 121, and the center core is struck up. This core is then blackened, slicked off, and baked. The cover plate is struck off with the stickers up, and baked so. This cover carries six 1-inch round holes through it, which will be just over the shell of the metal when the mold is closed. Five of them connect with the pouring basin and serve as runners, while the sixth serves as a riser.

Closing. In assembling the mold for pouring, the core is first set on a level bed of sand, the cope is accurately closed over it by the aid of the guide marks, and lastly the cover plate is closed in position. Now the whole mold is firmly clamped by blocking under the spider, from which wrought-iron loops or strings connect under the lugs of the building plate, as shown in Fig. 122.

The small core for the nozzle is now set, resting on stud chaplets. The cover plate D is slid over the end of this core and thus holds it firmly in position.

The casing is now placed around the mold and molding sand rammed in to support the bricks against the casting pressure. At the level of the nozzle core cinders are placed, and a pipe leads off to carry away the vent gases. The sand is rammed to about 12 inches over the cover plate and in it are cut the channels connecting the pouring basin and runners. A couple of bricks are set in the bottom of the basin to receive the first fall of metal from the ladle.

Pouring. In pouring, the runners must be flooded at once and kept so until the mold is full.

In heavy cylindrical castings it was formerly thought necessary to carry the shell of the casting some 6 inches higher than the top flange. This head served to collect all dirt and slag that perchance entered the mold with the iron, and it was cut off in the machine shop and returned to the foundry as scrap. With the increased knowledge of iron mixtures this head is now done away with in most instances.

Where a large casting is to finish practically all over, and very clean metal is therefore necessary, overflow channels, connecting with pig beds, are often constructed in modern practice. Then, when pouring, the metal is not stopped until a certain per cent of it has been flowed entirely through the mold. This of course tends to wash out any dirt which may have gotten into the mold when pouring began.

When the casting is cold, the casing and packing sand as well as the blocking under the spider are removed. Then the whole mold is carried to the cleaning shed where the bricks are removed and the casting cleaned.

Intricate Mold. As an example of a complex piece of loam work, let us consider the molding of a modern marine-engine cylinder, as shown in section, Fig. 123. The example given is that of a double-ported low-pressure cylinder of a triple-expansion type. In this case a full wooden pattern should be built, with core boxes for the various dry-sand cores that enter into the construction of the mold.

Foundation. The limits of this article prevent a detailed discussion of this subject; we will, therefore, confine ourselves mainly with an explanation of the drawing, Fig. 123. The heavy building plate has a spindle opening somewhat to one side of its middle to be under the center of the cylinder. Upon this building plate the foundation of the mold is swept, carrying the seat for the cope ring, the bottom face of the flange, and the seat for the main cylinder core. The cope ring *1* is made wide enough on one side to carry that part of the mold forming the steam chest. The main cylinder core *2*, the construction of which has already been explained, is next swept-up and lifted away, finished, and baked.

Cope. Now the cope ring is seated, and the mold built and struck off for the bottom of the steam chest on a level with the bottom face of flange. Then the pattern may be set. Its position is accurately determined by the main cylinder print and the smaller prints of the steam chest which are bedded into the loam in accordance with measurements along a radial line marked off on the loam surface. With the pattern well oiled, the cope is built to the height of the upper flange of the cylinder; the entire back of the steam-chest core print being left open. The top of the steam chest is lifted off with the drawback *3*, which joints at the middle of the upper steam nozzle, and carries that part of the mold to the level of the main cope joint. The two steam nozzles and the exhaust nozzle may be made with separate cores as explained in *D,* Fig. 122. By using the drawback, the entire top of the chest core print is left open for convenience in setting the chest and port cores.

The top of the cylinder is jacketed, and through it pass the stuffing-box and manhole openings. The flanges of these two openings connect and in the pattern are left loose. The whole top surface is so irregular that it requires three levels of sticker plates to mold it, aside from two small cover plates over flanges.

Covers. To the main cover *4 4 4 4* with its various lengths of fingers, is bolted a crab *5 5 5* to carry the loam below the flanges of the stuffing box and manhole; and below this again are hung the dry-sand cores, *8 8 8*, forming the jacketed part of the cylinder head. On top of the main cover is fastened a separate plate, *6*, to shape the top of the upper steam inlet. And at *7* a plate with wrought-iron bars cast along its edge carries the loam back of the steam-chest flange. The small cover plates, *9* and *10*, allow the flanges to be drawn for the parts which they mold.

The pattern is made in many parts so as to properly draw from the mold. When this has been done, all mold surfaces are carefully blackened and slicked before baking.

Coring. While the mold proper is being built, the dry-sand cores should be made up by the core makers, with the necessary rods, hangers, vent cinders, etc., as described under Core Making.

The manhole core, *11,* is made with a stop-off piece in the box to give the proper angle at the bottom of the core. It is hung to the cover and clears the main core by $\frac{1}{8}$ inch. The stuffing-box core rests in a print in the main cylinder core, and is held by a taper print in the cover plate *10.*

The jacket cores are hung as shown. The openings made in the loam above the crab, to allow the hook bolts to be drawn up tight, are stopped off with green sand as previously described. The inlet cores *12 12,* the exhaust core, *13,* and the lightening cores, *14 14 14,* are all bolted directly through the steam-chest core, *15,* to horizontal bars which are long enough to bear against the sides of the mold at the back. The upper inlet core, *12,* is kept from lifting under the pouring strain by being bolted to the body of the main cylinder core. Stud chaplets are also set between the inlet and exhaust cores to ensure correct thickness of metal at these points.

Venting. The vent is taken off from the main cylinder core through the stuffing-box core at the top. Sometimes a small ladleful of metal is poured through this opening, when the piece is being poured, to ensure lighting these gases. The vent for the series of port cores is taken off by ramming a cinder bed up the entire back of the steam-chest core, allowing the gases to escape at the top. For safety, also, vents are taken from the bottom of the port and chest cores by the usual pipe vent.

Pouring. The provision for pouring this mold requires especial attention. Notice the construction of the main basin, *16.* The long runner *17,* leading to the bottom gate, is left open on one side when the mold is built, so that it may be easily finished and kept free from dirt. Its open side is closed by cover cores when the mold is rammed up.

Ten or twelve small gates like *18* are connected with the pouring basin, by semicircular channels, but are so placed that no metal shall fall on a core. With the basin arranged as shown, the bottom part of the mold is first flooded with iron. When this has been done, the metal is poured in faster, so that hot iron is well distributed around the shell of the casting through the small top gates. Should the mold be poured at first from these top gates, the fall of the iron through the full height of the cylinder to the lower flange might result in cutting the loam on that surface.

Molds of this size are usually rammed in a pit so as to bring the pouring basin conveniently near the floor. The portion above the floor level is, of course, rammed inside a casing, as described in the previous example.

To guard against uneven cooling strains in this intricate casting, the clamping pressure on the mold is relieved when the metal has solidified, but the sand is not removed from around the brickwork for several days. This allows very gradual even cooling.

It will be noticed that the piston does not work directly upon the inner walls of this type of cylinder. A separate hollow shell or lining is cast of strong tough iron. This has outside annular ribs at top and bottom and middle, which are turned to fit correspondingly projecting ribs seen on the inside of the casting just under consideration. An air space is thus left between the lining and main casting which forms a jacket around the bore of the cylinder.

270 Moulds made by one man in 6 hours on the Tabor Moulding Machine at P. & F. Corbin Plant, New Britain, Conn.

FOUNDRY WORK

PART II

CASTING OPERATIONS

MELTING

General Characteristics. The subject of melting the metal which is to be poured into molds is one of the most important considerations in the foundry. It is also one which has received much attention in the last few years, the endeavor being to get away from the old rule-of-thumb methods and to arrive in the iron foundry at something near the precision in resulting metal that is already attained in the brass shops or the steel foundry.

The heat for all melting is obtained from practically the same two chemical elements—carbon, and oxygen—carbon coming from the fuel, be it coal, coke, oil, or gas; and oxygen coming from the air of the blast

The design of the furnace, the kind of fuel used, and the application of the blast vary in accordance with the peculiar properties of the different metals and the degree of heat required to melt them.

The melting of steel, copper alloys, and malleable cast iron will be dealt with under separate headings. We shall now consider only the melting of gray foundry irons.

CUPOLA FURNACE

Furnace Parts. Foundry iron is melted in direct contact with the fuel in a cupola furnace. The name was derived from the resemblance of the furnace to the cupola formerly very common on the top of dwelling houses.

Bottom. The cupola consists of a circular shell of boiler plate, lined with a double thickness of fire brick and resting on a square bedplate, with a central opening the size of the inside of the lining. This bottom is supported some $3\frac{1}{2}$ feet above a solid foundation, on four cast-iron legs. The bottom opening may be closed by cast-iron doors, which swing up into position, and are held so by an upright

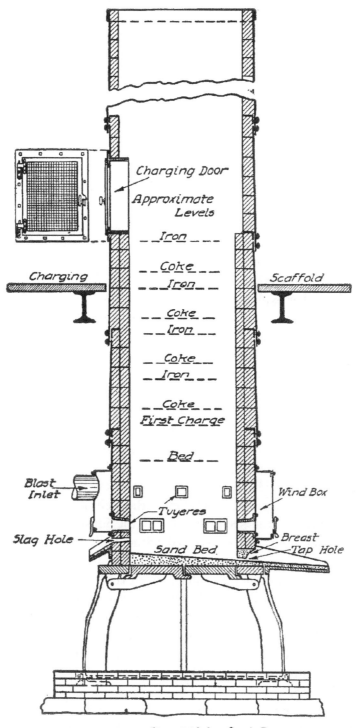

Fig. 124. Section Through Modern Cupola Furnace

iron bar placed centrally under them. These doors, protected by a sand bed, support the charge during the heat, and drop it out of the furnace when all the iron has been melted. The legs curve outward and the doors are hinged as far back as possible to protect them as much as can be from the heat of this "drop".

Breast. At one side, level with the bottom, is the breast opening, at which place the fire is lighted, and in which the tap hole is formed for drawing off the melted metal. The spout, protected by a fire-sand mixture, projects in front of the breast and guides the metal into the ladles.

Slag Hole. On cupolas over 36 inches inside of the lining, a slag hole is provided, which is similar to the tap hole, and is placed opposite the spout and about 2 inches lower than the main tuyères. Fig. 124 shows a section through a modern cupola furnace, and needs but little further explanation.

Lining. In lining the stack, the layer next the shell is usually made of boiler-arch brick about the size of regular fire brick. These are set on end, and should be fitted as tightly together as possible, and laid in a thin fire cement, made of very refractory fire clay and fine sharp silica sand. The object is to fill every crevice with a highly refractory material. Specially made curved fire brick can be purchased for the inside lining, although some foundrymen use the arch brick for this lining as well. The lining over the tuyères is shaped to overhang them slightly, to prevent melted slag dropping into them during the heat. The lining burns out quickest about 22 inches above the tuyères, at what is practically the melting zone. The angle shelves riveted to the shell, as seen in the illustration, allow this section of the lining to be renewed without disturbing the rest of the stack.

Tuyères. The oblong air inlets, called tuyères, are placed about 12 inches above the bed, and connect with an air-tight wind box which surrounds the outside of the stack near the base. The tuyères direct the blast into the fuel, increasing the heat sufficiently to melt the charge. In the wind box, opposite each tuyère, is an air-tight sliding gate with a peephole, which allows the melter to look directly into the furnace.

In the larger cupolas a second set of tuyères is arranged about 10 inches above the main ones. They are used, when long heats are

TABLE III

Sizes of Cupola Furnaces

Diameter Inside of Lining (inches)	Cupola Height (feet)	Charging Door Size (inches)	Melting Capacity	
			Per Hour (tons)	Per Heat (tons)
18	6 to 7	15 by 18	$\frac{1}{4}$ to $\frac{3}{4}$	1 to 2
20	7 to 8	18 by 20	$\frac{1}{2}$ to 1	2 to 3
24	8 to 9	20 by 24	1 to 2	3 to 5
30	9 to 12	24 by 24	2 to 3	4 to 10
40	12 to 15	30 by 36	4 to 8	8 to 20
50	15 to 18	30 by 40	6 to 14	15 to 40
60	16 to 20	30 by 45	8 to 16	25 to 60

run off, to make up for loss of wind caused by the main tuyères becoming partially choked by slag.

The height of the tuyères above the bed varies with the class of work to be poured. Where the metal is tapped and kept running continuously and is taken away by hand ladles, as in stove-plate work, the tuyères are as low as 8 inches or 10 inches above the bed; while in shops where several tons of metal may be required to fill one mold, the tuyères are as high as 18 inches above the bed. The height of the spout above the molding floor also varies in the same way; for hand-ladle work it may be but 18 inches above the floor, while a height of 5 or 6 feet may be required to serve the largest crane ladles.

Charging. Several feet above the bottom, there is a door in the side of the stack, through which the stock is charged into the furnace. A platform or scaffold is constructed at a convenient level below the charging door, and all stock is charged into the cupola from this platform. It should be at least large enough to store the stock for the first two charges of fuel and iron.

Table III, prepared by Dr. Edwin Kirk, gives the approximate height and size of charging door and the practical melting capacity of cupolas of different diameters.

Blast. *Fan Blower.* Blast for the cupola is furnished by either a fan blower or a pressure blower. Fig. 125 shows a modern fan blower, of which the blast wheel is detailed at A. The high speed of the blades forces the air, by centrifugal action, away from the center of the shaft. The casing is so designed that the blades cut

FOUNDRY WORK

TABLE IV

Fan-Blower Performance

Fan Diameter (inches)	Speed (revolutions per minute)	Wind Pressure (ounces per square inch)
18	4100	5
24	3750	6
36	2900	10
48	2600	14

off, as it were, at the top of the main outlet, the air being thus forced through the blast pipe. The current of air is continually being drawn into the fan through the central opening around the shaft.

Since air is very elastic, and the pressure in this case depends entirely upon the centrifugal action of the blades, should the tuyères

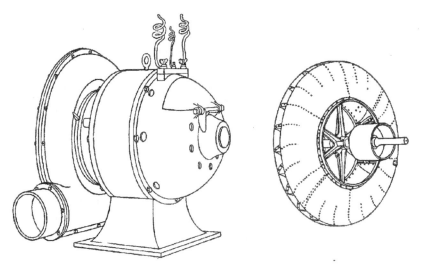

Fig. 125. Typical Fan Blower

become clogged, the amount of air forced into the furnace will be reduced proportionately. On the other hand, it requires less power to operate the fan with reduced area of outlet than it does when the discharge is open free.

An idea of the speeds at which blowers should run may be obtained from Table IV.

Pressure Blower. In the pressure blower shown in Fig. 126, the action is positive, as will be seen from the sectional view A,

114   FOUNDRY WORK

Fig. 126. The wipers mesh into each other in such a way that they entrap a quantity of air and force it out of the opening.

The full quantity of air is therefore forced through the tuyères at all times. In such case, the power necessary to operate the blower increases as the tuyères become choked, and the excessive force of the blast, due to choked tuyères, is hard on the lining of the cupola.

Gage. The cupola should have a blast gage attached to the wind box to measure the pressure of air which enters the tuyères. The

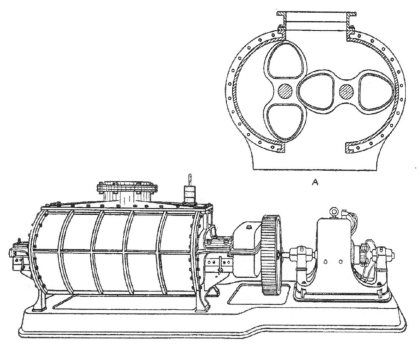

Fig. 126. Motor-Driven Pressure Blower

pressure should be sufficient to force the air into the middle of the cupola to insure complete combustion. The unit of air pressure is 1 ounce. From 8 to 16 ounces is approximately the range usual in cupolas of from 48 inches to 70 inches diameter, inside lining.

This pressure is measured by the displacement of water or mercury in a U-shaped tube. With both legs of the tube the same size, as in A, Fig. 127, the graduations represent the pressure of double that height of liquid. Such graduations would be as follows:

FOUNDRY WORK

With a water gage, a difference in levels of 1.73 inches corresponds to 1 ounce wind pressure, so that the scale graduations per ounce would be spaced

$$\frac{1.735}{2} = .865 = \frac{55}{64} = \frac{7}{8}\text{ in.} - \frac{1}{64}\text{ in.}$$

With mercury, a difference in levels of 0.127 inch corresponds to a pressure of 1 ounce so that the scale graduations would be spaced

$$\frac{0.127}{2} = .0635 \text{ in.} = \frac{1}{16}\text{ in.}$$

As this last spacing would be too small for practical use, mercury gages, as at B, Fig. 127, are made with an increased area exposed to the blast pressure, and are graduated accordingly.

Principles of Melting. Combustion cannot take place without oxygen, of which the air is the most abundant source of supply. For example, in the incandescent electric light, a strip of carbon is heated to a white heat, but it does not consume, or burn up, because all air has been exhausted from within the globe.

In the cupola furnace, both coal and coke are used as fuel. They consist largely of carbon, and, after being lighted by the kindlings, are kept at a glowing red heat by the natural draft through the open tuyères. The blast supplies the oxygen necessary for a melting heat. The quantity of air forced in by the blast cannot be

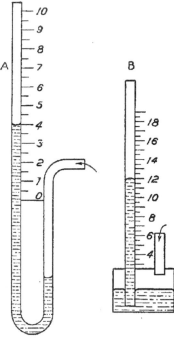

Fig. 127. Wind Gages

entirely taken up by the layers of fuel immediately above the tuyères; thus, complete combustion does not take place until a distance of 18 to 23 inches above the tuyères is reached. This is termed the *melting zone*. It is the aim of the melter to keep the top of his bed as nearly as possible at this level, so that the iron resting on it shall be exposed to this intense heat and melt rapidly. As the fuel of the bed burns away, this level tends to be lowered. But the iron on top of it melts and drops to the bottom of the cupola; and the subsequent charge of coke restores the level of the bed for the next charge of iron; and so on.

Cupola Operation

Running a Heat. The following routine must be pursued each time a heat is run off in the cupola:

(1) *Clear away* the dump from the former heat.

(2) *Chip out* the inside of the furnace with a special hand pick, removing the lumps of slag which collect about the lower part of the cupola walls, especially above the tuyères. Where the slag coating is comparatively smooth, do not touch it, as that is the best coating possible for the lining.

(3) *Daub up* with a mixture of fire sand, held together with about 1·4 fire clay, and, wet with clay, wash to a consistency of thick mortar. Smear the surface to be repaired with clay wash, then, using the hands, plaster the daubing mixture into the broken spots in the lining, being careful to rub it in well, especially about the tuyères. The top of the tuyères should be kept slightly overhanging.

The greater part of the daubing will be required from the bottom to the level of melting zone, about 22 inches above tuyères.

(4) *Swing up* the bottom doors, and support them by a prop of gas pipe.

(5) *Build the bottom;* first cover the doors with a 1-inch layer of gangway sand or fine cinders, then ram in burnt sand tempered about the same as for molds. This must be rammed evenly all over the bottom, and especially firm around the edges. The bottom should be made flat and level from side to side, with only a slight rise around the lining which should not extend more than 1 or 2 inches from the lining. The pitch varies with size of cupola; 1 inch to the foot will answer for cupolas of 24 inches to 30 inches diameter inside lining, while one-half that pitch will do for the larger furnaces.

The cupola bottom should be able to vent so that it will dry out quickly, and not cause the metal to boil before the furnace is tapped. It should be strong enough to hold its surface during the heat, but to break and drop at once when the bottom is dropped. Too much pitch causes excess of pressure on the bott, making trouble in botting

FOUNDRY WORK

up; with too little pitch the metal will not drain well, causing a tendency to chill at the tap hole. A little daubing mixture should be worked into the sand bottom just inside the tap hole, to prevent breaking at this point when the tapping bar is forced through.

(6) *Lay the fire* with shavings first, just inside the breast; then with fine kindling; then with enough large kindling to make sure of lighting a layer of coke sufficient to form the bed. When the gases from the lower part of the bed burn up through, showing that the fuel is well lighted, level up the bed with the addition of a little more coke.

(7) *The first charge* of iron should be put on now. Follow this with alternate charges of fuel and iron, to the level of charging door.

(8) *Form the tap hole;* lay a bar of iron about $\frac{7}{8}$ inch round in the spout, projecting in through the breast opening; fill in the breast around the bar with a strong loamy molding sand rammed hard. Recess this in well to leave the actual tap hole as short as possible.

(9) *Put on the blast* when ready for the metal, and leave the tap hole open. Bott up when the metal begins to run freely—generally about 7 minutes after blast is on.

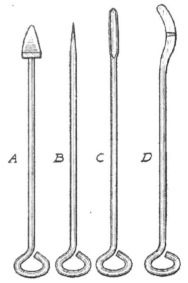

Fig. 128. Tapping Bars

Bott clay should be mixed with about $\frac{1}{8}$ sawdust, to make it more fragile when tapping, and is made up in small balls, and shaped onto the end of the bott stick *A*, Fig. 128.

(10) *Tap* when sufficient metal has collected to supply the first ladles.

The tapping bar *B*, Fig. 128, has simply a round taper point; *C* is a gouge or spoon-shape, useful for trimming sides of hole if the bott does not entirely free itself when tapped.

(11) *Drop the bottom*, when all the iron has been melted and run off. This is done by pulling away the bar that supports the bottom

TABLE V
Foundry-Ladle Data

	Hand Ladle		Bull Ladle		Crane Ladle		Geared Ladle	
Illustration	Fig. 129 A		Fig. 129 B, C		Like C, with bail		Fig. 130	
Control	Hand shank		Single or double hand shank		Bail with single or double hand shank		Worm gear on heavy bail	
Capacity (pounds)	30 50		80 350		300 2,000		1,000 35,000	
Weight (pounds)	15 16		35 100		115 350		1,900 7,000	
Dimensions (inches)	Inside Shell	Lining Thickness	Inside Shell	Lining Thickness	Inside Shell	Lining Thickness	Inside Shell	Lining Thickness
Top	7 to 8	$\frac{3}{4}$	9 to 15	$1\frac{1}{4}$	14 to 26	$1\frac{1}{4}$	20 to 75	2 to 4
Side	7 to 8	$\frac{1}{2}$	9 to 15	$\frac{1}{2}$ to $\frac{5}{8}$	14 to 26	$\frac{5}{8}$ to 1	20 to 60	1 to $4\frac{1}{2}$
Bottom	6 to 7	$\frac{1}{2}$ to $\frac{3}{4}$	8 to 13	$\frac{3}{4}$ to 1	12 to 23	1 to 3	18 to 66	$1\frac{1}{2}$ to

doors. Throw water on the dump by bucket or hose, to deaden the heat, and leave it to cool off over night.

Foundry Ladles. As the melted metal flows from the spout of the cupola, it is caught in ladles. The sizes of these are designated by the weight of metal they will hold; they vary from 30 pounds to 20 tons capacity.

Table V, containing references to Figs. 129 and 130, give compact data regarding foundry ladles.

The names of ladles relate to the method of carrying them. Hand ladles are made of cast iron or pressed steel. The larger ladles are built up of boiler plate. Cast iron is poured from the top of the ladle, which should therefore be provided with lips.

Lining. Ladles must be lined to protect them from burning through. Up to 1-ton capacity, the cupola daubing mixture is used. The bowl is smeared with thick clay wash, and the clay pressed in hard with the hands, being rubbed smooth on the inside. The lining should be kept as thin as possible, $\frac{5}{8}$ to $\frac{3}{4}$ inch on hand ladles, 1 inch to $1\frac{1}{2}$ inches on large ones; the bottom lining being from one-third to one-half thicker than sides, as it receives the first fall of the incoming metal.

The larger ladles are first lined with fire brick of thickness proportionate to their size, and then daubed on the inside with clay mixture similar to cupola lining. The lining must be well dried before use, to drive out moisture. In stove-plate and hardware shops, where most of the pouring is done with hand ladles, a special ladle drying stove similar to a shallow core oven is provided. A wood fire is built inside of the larger ladles to dry them out. To preserve a lining as long as possible, slight breaks are repaired daily. As with the cupola, the slag formed by the hot metal forms the best coating possible for the inside lining.

Pouring. The first thing to be considered in connection with pouring is skimming off the slag which collects on top of the metal. This should be done on the larger ladles before leaving cupola, and again while metal is being poured. For this, a long iron rod is used, with blade shaped as in *D*, Fig. 128. This is rested

Fig. 129. Hand and Bull Ladles

across the top of the ladle near the lip, and effectively holds the slag back; the long handle permits the skimmer to stand well back from the heat of the metal. On small ladles, skimmers are of course shorter, and the end is bent up more, for convenience, as the ladles will be much nearer the floor when pouring with them.

Hand and bull ladles are shown in Fig. 129, while Fig. 130 shows a crane ladle.

General Precautions. Much skill is required in pouring a mold. A molder must know the character of the work, and judge whether it must be poured fast or slowly. In general, light work cannot be poured too fast. Heavier work is poured more slowly. Care must be exercised to keep the stream steady from the first, and not to spill into the mold, as this may cause cold-shuts or leave shot iron in the castings. The runner basin must be kept full, for gates and runners are made with this express purpose in view, as has been stated previously.

Metal must not be allowed to chill or freeze in the ladle, as this would destroy the lining when it came to removing the cold metal. Metal left in the ladles when the mold is full, must be poured back into a larger ladle or emptied into a convenient pig bed. These latter are built in a sand bed usually near the cupola; or stout cast-iron pig troughs or chills are provided. The chills should taper well on the inside, holding about 60 pounds each. Some are arranged to swing on trunnions for convenience in dumping. They should be smeared with a heavy oil and dusted with graphite, to prevent the metal stick-

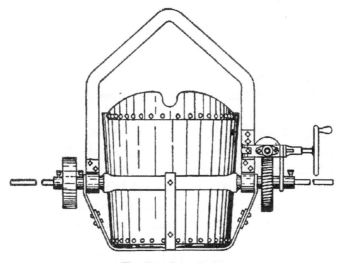

Fig. 130. Crane Ladle

ing in them. It is safer to heat these pig molds as well, so that no moisture will form and cause a kick or explosion when hot metal is first poured into them.

Cupola Mixtures

Requirements. By the term *cupola mixture* is meant the proportioning of the various pig irons and the scrap that make up cupola charges, with the object of obtaining definite physical and chemical properties in the resulting castings.

The requirements of castings vary; and metal that would be good if run into thin stove plate, would be entirely too soft for heavy machine castings. Again, iron that might answer all requirements of a bed plate would not be strong and tough enough for steam-cylinder work. The one in charge of this work, therefore, must so mix the different irons that his castings shall be soft enough to machine well if necessary, and at the same time be hard enough to stand the wear and tear of use.

Precision Essential. Formerly the appearance of the fracture of a pig or of scrap was the sole guide in determining mixtures. Unquestionably the fracture of iron indicates to the experienced eye much as to its physical properties, but this method of mixing has repeatedly proved misleading.

Representative practice today recognizes chemical analysis of the various irons as most essential to the proper mixing. Many firms now buy their pig iron and many other allied supplies by specification; and the chemical analysis of the iron must show that its various metalloids come within certain limited per cents.

To understand, then, these modern methods, we must consider the subject of the chemistry of iron

Affecting Elements. By the chemical definition, an element is a form of matter which cannot be decomposed, or, in other words, cannot be broken up into other forms by any means known to science.

Iron is such an element; but absolutely pure iron is of no commercial value; it is only when it is combined with impurities—or, as we must recognize them, other chemical elements—that mankind is interested in it.

In the forms of iron with which we are dealing—pig iron, and cast iron—five elements are considered as affecting their physical properties. These elements are carbon, silicon, sulphur, phosphorus, and manganese.

Carbon. Carbon is the most important and most abundant of all the chemical elements. It forms the principal part of many substances in daily use about us, such as coal, coke, lead pencils, graphite facings, etc.

In its relation to iron, carbon is peculiar in that it occurs in iron in two forms. One is in a chemical combination forming a hard substance with a fine grain, of which tool steel is the purest type. The other is simply a mechanical mixture forming minute facets of free carbon interposed between the crystals of the combined form. It softens cast iron, but weakens it by causing larger crystals to form. In drawing the finger across a freshly cut surface or fracture of cast iron, some of this free carbon may be rubbed off, and shows as dirt on the finger. We shall use the term *graphite* in referring to this form of free carbon, and the term *combined carbon* in referring to the element in its combined state.

Silicon. Silicon, of itself, is a hardening element in cast iron, but on account of its marked influence upon carbon formations, it is usually considered a softener. During the cooling process, silicon retards the formation of combined carbon, thus increasing the formation of graphite in proportion to the increase of silicon. At the same time, through its own influence on iron, it preserves the fine character of the grain, and so maintains the strength of the casting. In other words, within certain limits, the addition of silicon softens castings without impairing their strength. It makes iron run more fluid, and reduces shrinkage. Silicon varies in castings from 1.50 to 2.50 per cent.

Sulphur. Sulphur is the most injurious element in iron. It makes castings hard, red-short, and tends to the formation of blowholes. At the melting temperature, iron absorbs sulphur from the fuel—a decided reason why foundry coke should be as free as possible from this element. Sulphur in castings should not exceed 0 07 per cent.

Phosphorus. Phosphorus tends to make iron run very fluid when melted. It is a hardener. For machine castings it should not exceed 1 per cent.

Manganese. Manganese strengthens, and, of itself, hardens iron. Chemists are beginning to consider its proportions more carefully, in the belief that under certain conditions it acts as does silicon, softening the castings while retaining their strength. It is usual to keep it below 0 50 per cent.

Factors of Quality. The strength of a casting and the finish which it is capable of taking are largely dependent upon its having a fine even grain. We have seen that the porportions between the combined carbon, the graphite, and the silicon have decided influence upon this condition. But the rate of cooling must also be taken into account. A thin casting cools rapidly, tends to increase the combined carbon, and, without the influence of silicon, would be hard and brittle. In a heavy casting, the metal stays liquid longer, more graphite is thrown off, and the casting is naturally softer. Therefore light work requires a larger proportion of silicon to counteract the effect of the rapid cooling than does larger work.

Chemical Analysis. Modern practice makes daily analysis for the two carbons, for the silicon, and the sulphur, occasionally testing for the other elements to see that they are kept within their safe limits. Silicon, however, is used as the guide for regulating mixtures.

Proportions of Silicon. The following shows good proportions of silicon for different classes of work:

Casting	Silicon (per cent)
Steam cylinders	1.70
Medium heavy work ($\frac{1}{2}$-inch to 2-inch thickness)	2.00
Light work (less than $\frac{1}{2}$-inch thickness)	2.50

A more complete analysis of results to be aimed for is:

Casting	Elements (per cent)			
	Silicon	Phosphorus	Sulphur	Manganese
Automobile cylinders	2.25	1.0	0.075	0.5
Corliss engine cylinders ($1\frac{1}{4}$- to $1\frac{1}{2}$-inch thickness)	1.20 to 1.70	below 0.1	below 0.095	0.5

To calculate for any result, we must first know the analysis of the irons to be used in making the charge. We shall consider silicon as the guide.

In keeping track of results, the proportion of silicon in the local scrap of an establishment can be accurately estimated. With miscellaneous machinery scrap, this is more difficult; the following, however, are safe estimates:

Casting	Silicon (per cent)
Small thin scrap	2.0 to 2.4
Large scrap ranges	1.50 to 2.0

Method. The analysis of pig iron is made from drillings taken from a fresh fracture. Between the very fine grain about the chilled sides of the pig and the very coarse grain in the center, average-sized crystals will be noticed in the fracture. It is here that the drillings for analysis should be made, as indicated in Fig. 131. About a ¾-inch flat drill is best to use, as it cuts a more uniform chip from the varying grades of pig than does a twist drill.

To determine the analysis of a carload lot of pig iron, the following method is employed: Select ten pigs which will represent an average of the close, medium, and coarse-grained iron in the car. These pigs should be broken, and drillings taken from the fresh fracture. The drillings from these ten fractures are thoroughly mixed together, and about 2 ounces by weight, or a large tablespoonful by measure, is sufficient for the chemical analysis. The result is taken as the average analysis of the carload.

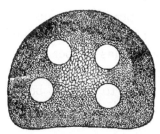

Fig. 131. Section of Pig Drilled for Analysis

The smaller foundries who do not employ a chemist can get a good working analysis of their iron from the furnace from which it is bought. Or, in many cases, sample drillings are sent to a practicing chemist.

Usual Silicon and Sulphur. The proportions of silicon and sulphur contained in the ordinary grades of pig iron are approximately as follows:

Grade of Pig	Silicon (per cent)	Sulphur (per cent)
Ferrosilicon	7 to 12	0.03
Silvery	3 to 5	0.03
No. 1 foundry	2.50 to 2.90	0.03
No. 2 foundry	1.95 to 2.40	0.04
No. 3 foundry	1.40 to 1.90	0.05

Calculation of Mixture. When we have the analysis of our iron, we can proceed to calculate the mixture, bearing in mind that some of the silicon will be burned out of the iron during the heat. From 0.15 to 0.25 per cent is a fair estimate for this loss in cupolas ranging in size from 36 inches to 72 inches inside lining. This loss must be deducted from the final estimate.

Illustrative Examples. It is proposed to make a mixture for miscellaneous machinery castings which require about 2 per cent of silicon, and we wish to use one-half scrap and three other irons, whose silicon contents are as follows:

Grade of Iron	Silicon (per cent)
Silvery	4
No. 1 foundry	2.65
No. 2 foundry	2.22
No. 3 foundry	1.75
Scrap	2.00

The student should bear in mind that per cent means $\frac{1}{100}$ or .01. To multiply a whole number by per cent, set the decimal point two places to the left in the percentage; thus 35 per cent of $5,000 = .35 \times 5,000 = 1,750$. In multiplying per cent by per cent, set decimal points in the percentages one place to the left before multiplying, and the result is expressed as per cent; thus 25% of $35\% = 2.5 \times 3.5 = 8.75$ per cent.

Then we may have the following proportions of silicon, using the above irons:

```
  (A)          (B)      (C)         (D)
  No. 1       25% × 2.65% = 0.6625%
  No. 2       20% × 2.22% = 0.4440%
  No. 3        5% × 1.75% = 0.0875%
  Scrap       50% × 2.00% = 1.0000%
                                    ─────────
  Total silicon content       = 2.194 %
  Deduct for loss in heat     = 0.20  %
                                    ─────────
  Estimated silicon in result = 1.994 %
```

Or, with No. 2 and silvery irons, we may have:

```
  (A)          (B)     (C)      (D)
  No. 2       45% × 2.22% = 0.999 %
  Silvery      5% × 4.00% = 0.200 %
  Scrap       50% × 2.00% = 1.000 %
                                   ─────────
  Total silicon content       = 2.199 %
  Deduct for loss in heat     = 0.17  %
                                   ─────────
  Estimated silicon in result = 2.029 %
```

In these examples, column (A) is the kind of iron; (B), per cent of this iron used in charge; (C), per cent of silicon in single grade of iron; (D), per cent of silicon to whole charge as supplied by each grade. One or more per cents in column (B) are usually decided upon before beginning calculations, and then the others are varied until the desired silicon content is obtained.

With this as a guide, it is a simple matter to find the actual weight for each grade, to make up any size of charge. For example, we wish to put 5,000 pounds on the bed and 3,000 pounds on other charges. Then, using the first mixture and the ratio 5:3 between the bed and the other charges, we have:

From column (B)	Bed	Other charges
No 1	$25\% \times 5,000 = 1,250$ lb	750 lb
No 2	$20\% \times 5,000 = 1,000$ lb.	600 lb.
No. 3	$5\% \times 5,000 = 250$ lb.	150 lb.
Scrap	$50\% \times 5,000 = 2,500$ lb	1,500 lb
Total iron	5,000 lb	3,000 lb.

Fuel. Both anthracite coal and foundry coke are used in the cupola. Coal, owing to its density, carries a heavier load than coke, but it requires greater blast pressure and does not melt as fast as coke.

Foundry Coke. Coke, for foundry use, should be what is known as "72-hour" coke, as free as possible from dust and cinders. Coke is made up of a sponge-like coke structure which is almost pure fixed carbon, and an open cellular structure, which makes it especially valuable as a furnace fuel because it is so readily penetrated by the blast

A representative analysis of a strong 72-hour coke is as follows·

Item	Proportion (per cent)
Moisture	0 49
Volatile matter	1 31
Fixed carbon	87 46
Sulphur	0 72
Ash	10.02
Cellular structure	50 04
Coke structure	49 96
Heat units per pound	12,937 B t u
Specific gravity	1 89

Proportions of Charge. The proportions of the bed fuel, the first charge of iron, and the subsequent charges of fuel and iron vary greatly with the size and design of the cupola, the grade of fuel used, and the method of charging. To determine the right amount of fuel for the bed, the most practical thing to do is to cut and try, especially with a new equipment.

For 36- to 48-inch cupolas, averaging 22 inches above the tuyères for the melting zone, with a 10-ounce blast to start, the best way to proceed is to chalk off this distance inside the cupola before daubing up. Then, from a ½-inch rod of iron, bend a shape like Fig. 132. The distance a equals the distance from the mark inside the cupola to about 4 inches above the bottom of the charging door. When the coke is well lighted, before charging the iron, level off the bed according to this gage. The safe practice is to have the bed too high. If the bed is too high, it is indicated by slow but hot metal; if the bed is too low, the metal is dull. After the first heat, the height may be adjusted until proper melting is obtained; then try always to work to the same height.

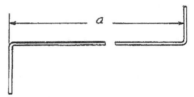

Fig. 132. Bed Gage

The weight and character of the coke charged on the bed should be carefully noted. The first charge of metal should be in the proportions of 2 pounds of metal to 1 of fuel; all others in the ratio of 10 of metal to 1 of fuel. Intermediate charges of coke should be just sufficient to preserve the upper level of the bed. The layer is usually about 6 inches thick; its weight should be carefully taken.

The action of the furnace must be carefully watched, with the object of making it melt the iron charged as rapidly as possible and of bringing it down white hot. Also, the ratio of iron to fuel should be reduced as low as may be, without sacrificing either of these other objects.

Supplementary Operations

Sand Mixing. When a mold is poured, the intense heat of the iron burns out those properties in the sand which give it its bond, making it necessary that a certain proportion of new sand shall be mixed with the heap sand and used as facing, as has been explained in earlier paragraphs.

The facing sand should be mixed daily for the molders by one or more of the laborers, at a place convenient to the storage sheds

128   FOUNDRY WORK

and molding floors. A hard smooth floor of clay or of iron plates is a great advantage.

The proportions of the different sands are measured by the shovelful, bucketful, or barrowful, and the sands are spread over each other in flat layers, sufficient water being sprinkled on to temper the pile. The sand then is cut through once with the shovel, is put through a No. 2 sieve, all lumps being broken up, and the refuse thrown

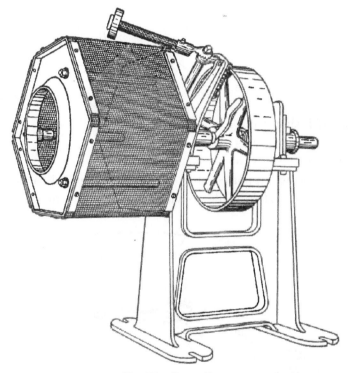

Fig. 133. Rotary Sieve

out is put through a No. 4 sieve, and finally is thrown in a pile ready for use.

When this work is done by hand, the ordinary screen sieve commonly employed by masons is used for the riddling, and a round foundry riddle for the final sifting. To reduce the labor of this, the riddle is slid back and forth on a pair of parallel bars supported conveniently above the storage pile.

Mixing Machines. The two classes of labor-saving machines used in mixing facings, core sand, etc., are those which mix by riddling; and those which mix by a combined breaking and stirring action. There are many varieties on the market, the illustrations shown being typical.

The rotary sieve shown in Fig. 133 is made with wire screen on the revolving sides, and is driven by belt or connected motor. Sand shoveled into the central opening is sifted in a pile on the floor, or directly into a barrow. The rubber hammer on top automatically raps each face of the sieve as it revolves, knocking the meshes free of sand.

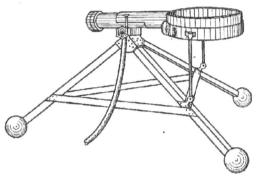

Fig. 134. Sand Shaker

Fig. 134 shows one of the latest labor savers in this line. Here a foundry riddle is supported in a metal ring attached to the piston of the machine. It is made to vibrate rapidly by means of com-

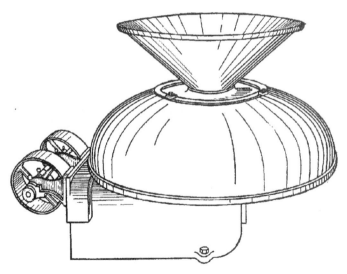

Fig. 135. Pulley-Driven Centrifugal Mixer

pressed air or steam. These shakers are made with portable tripod, as shown; they are also made stationary or are fastened on a post

130   FOUNDRY WORK

by means of a swivel joint, to be swung over a wheelbarrow or over a molding machine, and out of the way again when not in use.

Fig. 135 shows a centrifugal mixer. Inside of the umbrella casing, a horizontal plate about 12 inches in diameter and carrying a number of vertical steel pins about 6 inches long is fastened to the top of a short upright shaft driven by a belt running inside of the casing shown at the base of the machine. The machine runs about 1,500 revolutions per minute; and sand shoveled into the hopper is very evenly broken up by the pins and thrown against the steel hood, breaking and shattering any lumps of clay or loam and making a

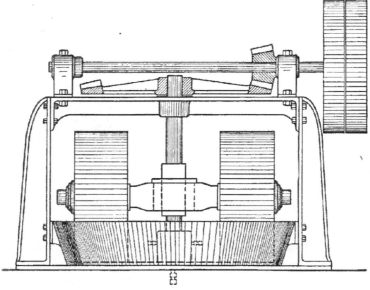

Fig. 136.   Facing Grinder

very uniform mixture. The hopper may easily be removed to clean the plate. The machine is used for the final mixing.

Fig. 136 shows a foundry grinder or facing mill. It is the type of mill used for mixing loam. Either the pan or the rollers are attached to the driving shaft and made to revolve, crushing and mixing whatever is shoveled into the pan. Frequently, a stout blade, something like a plowshare, is fixed between the rollers, and prevents the mixture caking to the bottom of the pan. The faces of the rolls are of very hard or of chilled cast iron to withstand wear. When the loam mixture is sufficiently ground, it must be shoveled from the pan, and delivered to the molders or stored temporarily. It will set if stored too long. This is the type of mill used in the steel foundries, for grinding the facing materials. The various sands are dumped into the pan at one side, and, when ground sufficiently, are shoveled directly from the pan into a centrifugal mixer. This prepares them for use.

Cleaning Castings. After a casting has solidified in the mold, the flash should be removed, leaving the casting in the sand. For light bench work and snap-flask work, the mold is lifted bodily and the sand dumped on the pile; the bottom boards are piled in one place, and the cases are piled in another ready for the next day's work. As the molds are dumped, the castings are removed from the sand and piled at the edge of the gangway. When all castings have been removed from the sand, the gates are broken and thrown in a pile by themselves. When cold enough to handle, the castings are removed to the cleaning room, and the gates and sprues are sent to the scrap pile. With heavier floor work, the clamps are

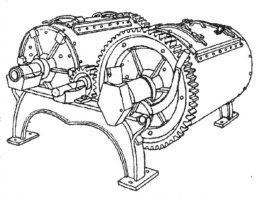

Fig. 137. Dustless Tumbling Barrel

removed as soon as the casting has set; the flash is rapped with a sledge hammer and is stripped off the mold, leaving the castings to cool gradually in the sand. Sometimes a sharp blow is given on top of the runner while it is still red; this breaks it off before the flask is shaken out. At a red heat, cast iron is very weak and can easily be broken.

Tumbling. The most effective way to clean small castings is in a rattling barrel. Fig. 137 shows a modern set of dustless barrels. The shell of the barrel is $\frac{5}{8}$-inch boiler plate riveted to cast-iron heads, with a door arranged to be entirely removed for packing and dumping. The bearings are hollow, and from one end the dust is drawn off through a galvanized-iron pipe. This pipe connects with an air-tight wooden chamber, as shown in Fig. 138, varying in size with the number of barrels connected with it. In this chamber hang a number of cloth-covered screens. An exhaust fan is connected to this chamber at the opposite end from the inlet pipe. When the fan is in operation, a strong current of air is drawn through the barrels and through the chamber. The dust, entering the chamber, settles on the screens, so that but little dust escapes to the outside air. When necessary, the exhaust is stopped, and, by means of a crank on the outside of the dust chamber, the screens are shaken and the dust drops off, when it can be removed through a trap into an ash can or wheelbarrow.

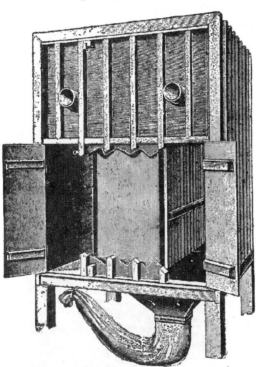

Fig. 138. Dust Collector for Tumbling Barrel

The driving shaft carrying the pinion revolves all the time, and any barrel may be thrown over into gear or drawn out of gear by the operation of a hand lever. The barrels should run about 25 revolutions per minute. Each barrel should be packed as full as possible with several shovelfuls of gates, shot iron, or hardened stars thrown in with the castings. The cleaning is accomplished in from 20 minutes to half an hour by the scouring action of castings, scrap, etc., rubbing against each other. Castings up to 50 or 100 pounds can be rattled, but only those of a similar character as to design or weight should be packed in together, otherwise the lighter castings will be broken by the heavier. When removed from the barrel, the work should show a smooth clean surface of an even gray color.

From the rattlers, castings go to the grinding room, where projecting gates or other slight roughness is removed on the emery wheel.

Heavy castings are cleaned by hand, by pickling, or by sandblasting.

Hand-Cleaning. When cleaning by hand, the worst of the sand is rapped off by light hammering, the remainder scraped off with old files and with steel-wire brushes such as that shown in Fig. 139. Some shops rub off finally with broken pieces of coarse emery wheel. Risers and fins are removed with cold chisels. The pneumatic chisel, shown in Fig. 140, is used as a timesaver. Where work is light enough to handle, small fins are removed by emery wheels; medium coarse wheels will cut faster on cast iron than fine ones, and will hold their shape better.

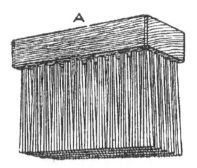

Fig. 139. Steel Bristle Brush

It is when castings must be cleaned by hand, that the value of a good facing dust shows itself. With the proper facing, the sand parts readily from the casting leaving a fine-looking smooth surface. With poor facings, on the other hand, the iron burns into the sand, making it hard to clean, and leaves a rough surface on the work.

Pickling. Pickling is a method of cleaning resorted to where there is much machining to be done on a casting. The work is placed in a pile on a suitable platform, and dilute sulphuric acid is thrown over it during one day, frequently enough to keep it well wet. The platform should be arranged to drain the acid back into the vat.

Fig. 140. Pneumatic Chisel for Cutting Risers and Fins

Acid is diluted from 1:8 to 1:10. After about 12 hours' bath with acid, the castings are washed clean with hot water. The acid acts on the hard skin of oxide of iron which forms when the iron strikes the damp sand, and it eats through this skin to the iron itself. The washing water should be hot enough to warm the castings sufficiently for them to dry rapidly without rusting. The acid must be thoroughly washed off, or it will continue to eat

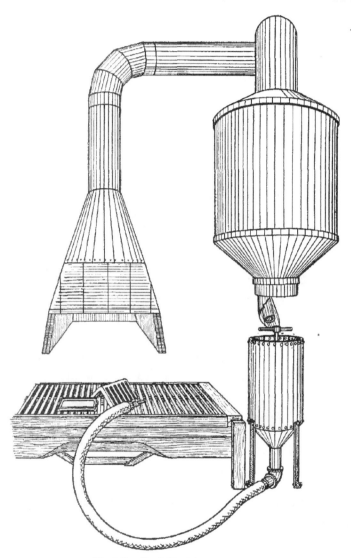

Fig. 141. Sand-Blast Arrangement

into the iron and cause a white powder—sulphate of iron—to form on the surface.

An excellent arrangement for a pickling department is to have the trough arranged on skids which allow it to be rocked endwise.

This drains into the pickling vat when acid is being thrown on, and into the gutter when the castings are being washed. Sheet lead is the best protective covering for small pickling troughs, but it is expensive and not durable enough to stand for heavy work.

Sand-Blasting. For castings of such shape and size that they cannot well be rattled, but are too small to be cleaned by hand, the sand blast has been used to advantage in many shops.

Fig. 141 gives an idea of the arrangement of the cleaning stall. Castings are placed on the wooden grating. By means of com-

Fig. 142. Core Rod Straightener

pressed air a sharp silica sand is forced through a strong rubber hose and is directed against the castings by a hardened-steel nozzle. The operator wears a helmet supplied with fresh air by an air hose, to protect his eyes and lungs from the clouds of fine dust. An exhaust hood is arranged also to take off as much of the dust as possible.

The manual labor of this method is practically reduced to nothing, aside from handling the castings. The system, however, requires the installation of a rather considerable equipment, which has debarred its use in many foundries.

Re-Use of Core Rods. In removing cores, the bars become very much bent. In such shape they were formerly scrapped, or refitted to suit new cores with a hammer and block of iron. Fig. 142 shows a very practical power machine which delivers the bars perfectly straight. The machine consists of a pair of rolls, with different sizes of grooves turned in them, which pull a rod through a flaring mouthpiece and deliver it through a corresponding eye on the opposite side. The machines are made in different sizes, and take rods from ¼-inch to ¾-inch diameter.

STEEL WORK

Present Development. This class of work has developed within the last few years, and, beginning with the heavier parts of marine and engine construction, it is now crowding the field of drop forgings. Steel castings are malleable, and are very much stronger than iron ones. The principles of molding involved are similar to those in other classes of molding, but practice is varied to meet special conditions.

Processes. The art of making steel castings may be divided into three heads: (1) preparation and melting of the metal; (2) making and pouring the molds, (3) heat-treatment of finished castings. As the first and third heads come more properly under other departments, we shall here simply outline these processes, dealing in detail with the second heading only.

Characteristics of Metal. This branch of foundry work has developed to a great extent since the early nineties. The metal is similar in mixture, method of melting, and physical properties to the steel which is poured into ingot molds for forging purposes. The graphitic carbon is entirely burned out; the strength of the metal is therefore very much greater than that of cast iron. Combined carbon, manganese, and silicon are the elements depended upon for this strength; sulphur and phosphorus are kept very low. A typical analysis shows these elements in the following proportions:

Carbon	Manganese	Silicon	Sulphur	Phosphorus
0.27%	0.85%	0.35%	0.020%	0.025%

Owing to the purity of this form of iron, about 50 per cent more heat is required to melt it than is necessary in the case of pig iron—or about 3,300 degrees Fahrenheit. When melted, the metal runs much more sluggishly than cast iron, and, on account of the absence of graphitic carbon, it does not expand at the moment of solidifying, and therefore does not take as sharp an impression. To insure as perfect an impression as possible, the molds are constructed with a good head of metal in the risers, and they are poured under pressure. The shrinkage is double that of iron; the risers are made very large, and are placed directly on the casting to insure feeding well. Great care must be exercised that neither mold faces nor cores bind during cooling, as such binding might cause a flaw.

Shrinkage. When two surfaces meet at right angles, the corner remains hot longest, and

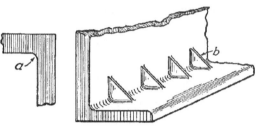

Fig. 143. Shrinkage Webs

the sides shrink away, tending to cause a fracture at *a*, Fig. 143. To overcome this, thin webs are cut by the molder about every 4 inches or 6 inches—shown at *b*. These cool first, and hold the adjacent sides in position, preventing them from pulling away from each other. The internal strain due to this cooling is relieved by the annealing. After the casting is annealed, the webs are cut away.

STEEL MOLDS

Facing Mixtures. To withstand the high heat, pure silica sand is used as the basis of the facing mixtures for steel molds. Pure quartz or silica rock is quarried, and reduced to sand form through a series of rock crushers. At the foundry the necessary bond is given by the addition of fire clay and molasses water. These are thoroughly mixed with the sand in a facing mill and mixer, Figs. 135 and 136. A typical mixture is as follows:

> 1 barrow silica sand
> 3 pails powdered fire clay
> Temper with molasses water

Where quartz sand is very expensive, the following mixtures, I, II, III, or IV, will reduce the cost. The old crucibles and fire brick should be crushed separately in the mill before mixing.

INGREDIENTS	PROPORTIONS			
	(Castings up to 2 In. Thick)		(Castings over 2 In. Thick)	
	(I)	(II)	(III)	(IV)
Old facing sand	8	12	1	
Old crucibles	2		10	
Fire brick	2		5	
Fire clay	2	1	3	1
Coke	1		1	
Silica sand		5		5
Graphite		2		
Tempering medium, molasses water				

For *facing wash*, these mixtures are ground very fine, and thinned with molasses water.

Core sand for steel work is practically the same mixture as the mold facing. For thin metal a somewhat less refractory natural sand may be added to reduce the cost of the mixture.

For *small round or flat cores*, $\frac{1}{20}$ part rosin, with silica sand, tempered with molasses water, makes a good core. It should, however, be thoroughly burnt.

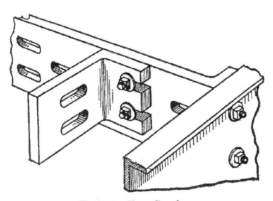

Fig. 144. Short Crossbar

For *core-wash* mixture, use 3 parts silica flour; 1 part Ceylon graphite; molasses water.

Flasks. Flasks for steel work are built of cast iron, Fig. 4, Part I. Full-length crossbars are bolted in the cope, 6 inches to 8 inches on centers, depending on the size of the flask. Short crossbars are fastened between these as needed, say 12 inches to 16 inches on centers, as seen in Fig. 144. Oblong bolt holes 4 inches on centers are cast in the sides of the flask and in all crossbars. Slots to correspond are cast in flanges of bars, so that they may be readily removed or shifted when fitting the cope to the pattern.

FOUNDRY WORK

The holes for pins should be drilled to template in all flasks of the same size, so that copes and drags may be interchanged. Flask pins are slipped through the holes temporarily when the flask is being closed or opened.

On large work the cope is bolted to the drag while being rammed. The bottom plate is of cast iron, and is clamped to the flange of the drag with short clamps and steel wedges. The same tools are used for packing and finishing the mold as those described in connection with iron molding.

Flasks of from 18 inches to 48 inches in length have two handles bolted on the ends to lift them with. Larger flasks have trunnions, rockers, or U-shaped handles cast on the sides.

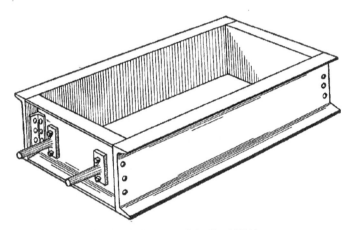

Fig. 145. Small Flask for Steel Molds

Fig. 145 shows type of convenient small flask built up of channel and angle iron, size 14 by 20 to 24 by 48 inches.

Packing. In packing the mold, place the pattern on the board and cover with $1\frac{1}{2}$ to 3 inches of facing, depending on the size of the job. Tuck well with the fingers. The facing is used as prepared by the mixer, not sifted. Set the drag on the board, shovel in heap sand, and ram the mold somewhat harder than for iron. Strike off, and seat the bottom plate, fastening it firmly to the flange of drag with clamps or bolts. When this is done, roll the mold over, and remove the moldboard.

Press with the fingers all over the joint surface, especially around the pattern, to make sure of firm packing. If soft places are found, they should be tucked in with facing sand. When needed repairs are made, slick the joint all over. Use burnt core sand for making the parting.

Try on the cope and adjust bars to fit the pattern. Clay-wash the cope before packing. Put on necessary facing over the joint and the pattern. Set the gate on the joint, but place risers directly on the pattern. Set the necessary gaggers, shovel in heap sand, and

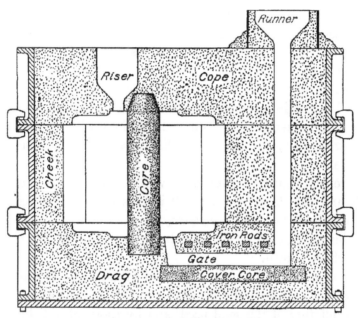

Fig. 146. Section Through Steel Mold

ram the cope. Vent well, lift the cope, moisten the edges, and draw the pattern.

In finishing the mold, nails are used freely, about $1\frac{1}{2}$ to 2 inches apart, driven in till the heads are flush with the surface of the sand. This is to prevent the cutting of the surface by the rush of hot metal when the mold is poured.

It is at this stage that the thin webs previously mentioned, are cut into the corner fillets where needed. The whole surface of the mold must be smoothly slicked over with the trowel and convenient slicks. When this is done, paint on the facing wash with a very flexible long-bristled brush.

FOUNDRY WORK

Fig. 146 shows the section of a mold for a shrouded pinion, and illustrates the points above mentioned. The runner is lead in at the bottom by use of a cover core, as described in Dry-Sand Molding.

Molds for steel should be more than dried; they should be thoroughly baked to drive off every particle of moisture. This prevents the steel boiling in the mold and causing imperfections in the casting.

Where but little machine work is to be done on small work up to $1\frac{1}{4}$ inches thick, the molds may be made up in wooden flasks and poured green. For this class of work, only pure quartz sand and fire clay are used, tempered with molasses water. These may be made up and poured on the same day.

Cores. Cores for steel molds are made up in boxes similar to those used in the iron foundry. Although using special sands, the cores are strengthened with iron rods, vented with cinders, and provided with convenient hangers for lifting, as described in previous paragraphs.

Where cores must be made in halves, one set of half-cores may be made and baked. The other half is then made and rolled over directly on the baked half. Fire-clay wash is used to cement the joint. This method allows the joint between the halves of a core to be nicely slicked down.

Steel cores must be more collapsible than those for iron, on account of the excessive shrinkage of the metal. This is provided for in the mixture of the sand used, and by thoroughly baking the core to reduce the effect of the binding materials to a minimum.

STEEL CASTINGS

Running a Heat. *Open-Hearth Melting.* The melting of steel is a science by itself, and cannot be dealt with adequately in an article of this character. Only a very brief description of the process is given.

The main feature is the difference in application of heat. Metal is melted in what is termed the open-hearth furnace, a sectional plan of which is shown in Fig. 147. The charge of scrap steel and pig iron is placed on the central hearth. Heat is obtained by producer gas supplied with air blast. Both gas and air are heated in one set of regenerators before entering the combustion chamber. The flame plays on top of the charge, and the waste gases pass off through the other regenerator section of the furnace, heating up its brickwork. The direction of the gases is changed about every 20 minutes. The regenerator is practically a tunnel about 15 feet long, filled with brickwork built up as shown in Fig. 148. About 4 heats a day are run from the furnaces.

Samples of the bath are analyzed at intervals during the heat. Guided by these analyses the proper proportions of ores, fluxes,

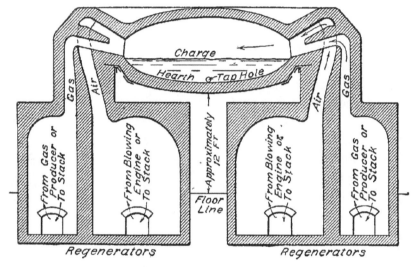

Fig. 147. Section through Open-Hearth Furnace with Regenerators

and pig are added to the bath to give it the right composition, a typical analysis of which has been given.

Pouring. When the bath is in proper condition, the entire charge, be it 5 tons or 40 tons, is drawn off into a ladle previously heated by a special gas burner. This ladle is lifted by the crane and carried to the pouring floor.

In order to secure the soundest metal free from pent gases or slag, all steel for casting purposes is tapped from the bottom of the ladle. The stopper is carried by a stiff round bar encased in fire-clay tubing. This passes through the liquid metal, as in Fig. 149, and may be raised or lowered by an arm attached to a rack-and-pinion mechanism bolted to the outer shell of the ladle and operated by means of a large hand wheel. The ladle is swung into position with the tap hole directly over the pouring head. Four men hold the ladle steady with long iron rods. The metal thus enters the mold under the head of pressure of all the steel above it in the ladle.

When all the steel is drawn from the ladle, the latter is swung on its side near the furnaces, the stopper is removed, and all the slag possible is racked out. The ladles must be repaired after each heat, often to the extent of replacing one-half of the thin fire-brick lining.

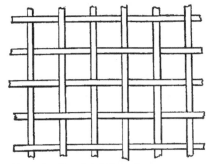

Fig. 148. How Brick Is Set in Regenerators

The casing of the stopper will last for but one heat, as the rod is sure to get bent out of shape. The rods are repaired by a blacksmith before recasing them.

Setting Up Molds. Setting up is usually done by a different set of men from those employed to make the molds.

For convenience in pouring, runner boxes, such as shown in Fig. 150, and which serve simply as funnel-shaped

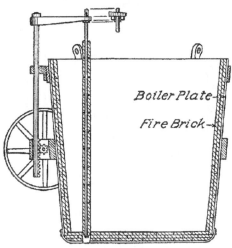

Fig. 149. Section of Steel Ladle

mouths to the runners, are rammed up in small round sheet-metal boxes, using a wooden pattern to form the hole. These are baked in the oven.

When the molds are properly dried, they should be removed from the oven, placed on the pouring floor, and have the dust blown out with compressed air.

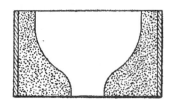

Fig. 150. Runner Box for Steel Mold

Now set the cores, close the molds, and clamp along joint flanges. Set runner boxes over the runners, and tuck heap sand around to prevent leakage. In pouring, a mold is filled only to the level of the top of the risers. The metal drains from the runner box, thus allowing it to be used more than once.

Cleaning Castings. Steel castings do not run as smoothly as cast-iron ones, but they have this advantage, that, if they show only slight surface defects, the metal may be peened over with a hammer to improve appearance. The intense heat makes the metal burn into the sand greatly, so that cleaning is much more difficult; and the sand often must be almost cut from the castings by means of long cold chisels, struck with sledges. Pneumatic hammers are used to a large extent in cleaning and in removing fins and slight projections. Where shrinkage webs show, they must be cut out. Steel does not break off as does cast iron. The heavy gates and risers must be

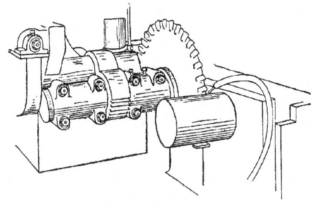

Fig. 151. Cutting Off Riser

removed by metal saws, as shown in Fig. 151, or by drilling a number of 1-inch holes side by side through the base of the riser and then breaking it off. The castings are generally annealed before the risers are cut off.

Annealing. In all steel castings of any size, cooling strains will develop on account of the shrinkage, and these should be relieved by annealing. In suitable trench-like ovens, the steel is heated to a dull redness. This allows the grain to assume normal conditions. The heating is usually done with a wood fire. Overheating renders the grain coarse, and weakens the casting. As indicated by the following figures, proper heat-treatment materially increases strength and toughness, and the work which is properly annealed is not only actually stronger, but being tougher, will stand more hard usage.

Conditions	Tensile Strength (lb per sq in.)	Elongation (per cent)	Reduction of Area (per cent)
Raw	80,360	13 31	16 2
Annealed	81,767	27 6	40 4
Improperly annealed	79,421	14 3	17 8

MALLEABLE PRACTICE

Development. It is believed that early attempts to soften hard castings by reheating them, and the collection and publication of the results of these operations in 1722, by Réaumur, which led to the taking out of patents on the process by Lucas in 1804, comprised the early history of the malleable-iron industry

Seth Boyden of Newark, New Jersey, produced the first malleable iron in America It is recorded that in 1828, The Franklin Institute of Philadelphia, Pennsylvania, awarded him a premium for the best specimens of annealed cast iron. These were mainly harness trimmings

Before 1890, the secrets of the process of malleableizing were closely guarded, which accounts for its slow growth, but since then great advances have been made both in quality and tonnage, due to a better knowledge of the principles involved. As the industry now stands it is farthest advanced in the United States. It is estimated that for the year 1907 the output for all Europe was but 50,000 tons as compared with a production of 980,000 tons in America for the same year.

It is rather surprising that, while there is more skill required to produce malleables—and there are several extra operations—the price is so little in advance of that for gray iron. This is accounted for in part by the large number of castings ordered from a given pattern

Comparative Characteristics of Metal. An idea of the value of this material is best obtained by a comparison of its properties with those of similar substances Thus, gray-iron castings range from those nearly black in fracture, to white, with all degrees of softness up to glass hardness. They may be strong or weak and still serve their purpose. The desirable characteristics of the gray-iron casting is its extreme resistance to compression. Where great shock is to be cared for, great massiveness is required.

The steel casting has the highest strength of any cast metal; it may be deformed considerably without danger, and is cheaper than a corresponding forging.

The malleable casting is the connecting link between the two above mentioned. It is stronger than the gray casting but not as strong as cast steel. It can be bent or twisted considerably without breaking, and approaches gray iron in compressive strength; but its most valuable characteristic is resistance to shock. This property is best illustrated by the car coupler, a large number of drop tests having shown the value of the malleable coupler as compared with one of cast steel.

TESTING

Methods. There are two general ways for testing malleable cast iron: (1) by so-called shop tests; and (2) by laboratory tests of bars cast from every heat and annealed with the castings.

Shop Tests. The usual shop tests consist of bending occasional castings, as well as of twisting the longer pieces, and also of the making and breaking of test wedges. These wedges are about 6 inches long and 1 inch square for 3 inches of their total length, then tapering down in thickness to nothing for the last 3 inches, but keeping the full inch width; this gives thick iron as well as thin on the same piece. When the test wedges come from the annealing, they should be broken on an anvil by striking them with short light blows, the object being to see how much the thin end of the wedge can be bent before the piece breaks, after which, by holding the two parts together and observing the bend, a very fair idea of the quality of the castings these wedges represent, may be had.

Laboratory Tests. The regulation test bars are rectangular in form and are of two sizes. the 1-inch square bar to represent castings $\frac{1}{2}$ inch thick and over, while a 1- by $\frac{1}{2}$-inch section bar cares for the lighter castings.

The following specifications adopted by the American Society for Testing Materials form the only official standard in existence.

Specifications for Malleable Cast Iron

Process of Manufacture. Malleable-iron castings may be made by the open-hearth, air-furnace, or cupola process. Cupola iron, however, is not recommended for heavy or important castings.

Chemical Properties. Castings for which physical requirements are specified shall not contain over 0.06 per cent of sulphur or over 0.225 per cent of phosphorus

Physical Properties. (1) *Standard Test Bar.* This bar shall be 1 inch square and 14 inches long, cast without chills and left perfectly free in the mold. Three bars shall be cast in one mold, heavy risers insuring sound bars.

Where the full heat goes into the castings, which are subject to specification, one mold shall be poured 2 minutes after tapping into the first ladle, and another mold shall be poured from the last iron of the heat

Molds shall be suitably stamped to insure identification of the bars, the bars being annealed with the castings. Where only a partial heat is required for the work in hand, one mold shall be cast from the first ladle used and another after the required iron has been tapped.

(2) Of the three test bars from the two molds required for each heat, one shall be tested for tensile strength and elongation, the other for transverse strength and deflection. The other remaining bar is reserved for either tensile or transverse test, in case of failure of the other two bars to come up to requirements. The halves of the bars broken transversely may also be used for the tensile test.

(3) Failure to reach the required limit for the tensile test with elongation, as also for the transverse test with deflection, on the part of at least one test, rejects the castings from that heat

(4) *Tensile Test* The tensile strength of a standard test bar for casting under specification shall not be less than 40,000 pounds per square inch. The elongation measured in 2 inches shall not be less than $2\frac{1}{2}$ per cent.

(5) *Transverse Test.* The transverse strength of a standard test bar on supports 12 inches apart, pressure being applied at the center, shall not be less than 3,000 pounds with deflection at least $\frac{1}{2}$ inch

Test Lugs. Castings of special design or special importance may be provided with suitable test lugs at the option of the inspector. At his request, at least one of these lugs shall be left on the casting for his inspection.

Annealing. (1) Malleable castings shall neither be over- nor under-annealed. They must have received their full heat in the oven at least 60 hours after reaching that temperature.

(2) The saggers shall not be dumped until the contents shall be at least black hot.

Finish. Castings shall be true to pattern, free from blemishes, scale, or shrinkage cracks. A variation of $\frac{1}{16}$ inch per foot shall be permissible. Founders shall not be held responsible for defects due to irregular cross-sections and unevenly distributed metal

Inspection. The inspector representing the purchaser shall have all reasonable facilities given him by the founder to satisfy him that the finished material is furnished in accordance with these specifications. All tests and inspections shall be made prior to shipment

In general it may be said it is not necessary to have a metal very high in tensile strength but rather one which has high transverse strength and good deflection. This means a soft ductile metal which adjusts itself to conditions more readily than a stiff strong product, for it is very hard to produce a strong and at the same time soft material, especially in the foundry making only the lighter grades of castings.

PRODUCTION PROCESSES

Preparing Molds

Patterns. One of the most important departments of the malleable works is the pattern shop. Malleable castings are comparatively light when considered in connection with general gray-iron practice and many times are ordered in enormous quantities from the same pattern.

Every refinement in pattern-making for light castings is found in this branch of the foundry industry. When developing a new article, the pattern-maker must practically live in the foundry. As trial castings are made he must measure them up with the pattern and make changes as found necessary; he must try them out again both before and after annealing, and with iron from different parts of the heat, and thus bring out new points calculated to help the molder and to lessen difficulties from shrinkage. It is the rule never to start an order for a quantity until the pattern has been tried out, the hard castings have been broken for evidence of shrinkage, and everyone has been satisfied it is safe to proceed.

Construction Difficulties. The terms shrinkage and contraction, as applied to malleable castings, should be clearly understood before any further mention is made of this subject. While *shrinkage* in gray-iron practice is often considered as the shortening of a casting in cooling, in malleable practice shrinkage means the tearing apart of the particles of iron in the interior of a larger section, close to a small one, leaving a spongy mass which is weak and very dangerous to the life of a casting. *Contraction* being simply reduction in size while the casting is cooling, amounts roughly to $\frac{1}{4}$ inch per foot in the hard, i.e., before annealing. During the annealing, about half of this is recovered, so that the net result is about the same as in gray-iron practice. It should be plain, however, that this big contraction causes the tearing as above mentioned when there are heavy sections which remain in a molten state a little longer than do adjoining light sections, unless liquid iron can be fed in. Where this is impossible, the use of chills must be resorted to and fillets made much larger.

In gating patterns it is to be remembered that white iron chills easily and must be poured rapidly. To a certain extent, this limits the number of pieces that may be run successfully, unless the gates be made so large there would be danger of dirty castings. The runners should be large and the sprues heavy, the idea being to get a large amount of metal in front of the gate for the individual casting.

The use of the match plate is largely resorted to also, as being well adapted to this class of work. Fig. 152 shows a group of three of the gated patterns in daily use in the Arcade Malleable Iron Foundry, Worcester, Massachusetts. In Fig. 153 there are shown 84 small thumb nuts on one gate; also 18 hinge patterns mounted on a match plate.

Fig. 152. Gated Patterns

Molding Methods. But little difference from ordinary gray-iron methods, occurs in molding practice other than in gating and in pouring. Since white iron melts at a somewhat lower temperature, there is less danger of sand burning into the casting, so less attention is paid to facing sand.

A large per cent of the work is made in the snap flask on the bench, as illustrated in Fig. 154. From the fact that nearly all work is in quantity, here is where molding machines may be used to great advantage. As these are explained elsewhere, no more need be said except that care should be exercised in the selection of types

150 FOUNDRY WORK

Fig. 153. Typical Gated Pattern and Match Plate

Fig. 154. Molds in Position for Pouring

FOUNDRY WORK

Fig. 155. View of Molding Floor, Fig. 154, Taken from Opposite End of Plant

Fig. 156. Sand-Mixing Machine
Courtesy of Standard Sand and Machine Company, Cleveland, Ohio

best suited to local conditions. Fig. 155 is a view from the opposite end of the same foundry floor.

Flasks. While much of the work is handled in snap flasks, it is not unusual to find metal flasks closely conforming to the shape of the pattern, thereby greatly reducing the amount of sand to be handled, with a corresponding reduction in cost of production.

Cores. Practically all castings are cored and the problem is to produce a sufficient number of cores that there may be no delay for the molder. As there is no important difference in the preparation of cores—the same sand and binders being used—the large number required warrants the introduction of modern sand-handling and mixing machinery to a somewhat greater extent than in gray iron.

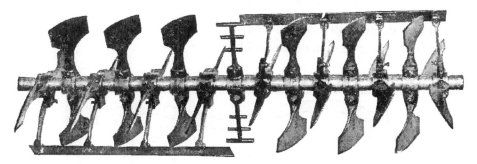

Fig. 157. Mixing Paddles of Standard Sand-Mixing Machine

The batch mixer alone proves of great value by the reduction of binder required due to its more even distribution; oftentimes this amounts to nearly 100 per cent. The type of batch mixer shown in Fig. 156 is made by the Standard Sand and Machine Company, Cleveland, Ohio. Fig. 157 is a view of the mixing paddles.

Melting Metal

Methods of Melting. Under this head the several methods in use will be described, which are as follows: (1) crucible; (2) cupola; (3) air-furnace; and (4) open-hearth.

Crucible Melting. The quality of metal produced by this method is without doubt of the best. Being melted out of contact of the fuel, there is no danger of absorbing impurities therefrom, but the small amount of metal available at one time limits the production to only the smaller work. Partly for this reason, the excessive cost of production does not admit of competition with other methods which, while lacking somewhat in quality, yet meet actual requirements.

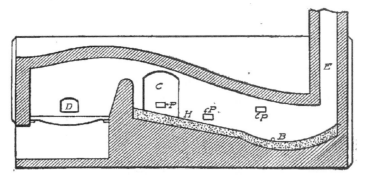

Fig. 158. Air Furnace with Bath at End Remote from the Bridge

A more detailed description of melting in the crucible is given in the subsequent section on Brass Melting.

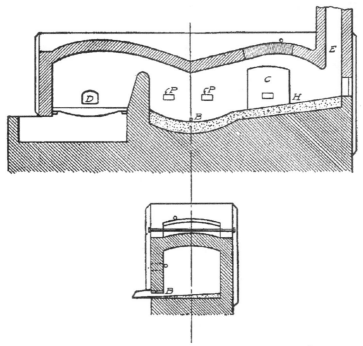

Fig. 159. Longitudinal Section of Air Furnace with Bath Immediately behind the Bridge

Cupola Melting. As in gray iron, the cupola offers the most economical method of melting iron, not only in cost of installation and saving of fuel, but in ease of manipulation as well. It has some disadvantages which restrict its use, the greatest being the inferior quality of metal produced, which is caused by the contact of metal with the fuel, and also the danger of burned iron which in turn makes sluggish iron, with the result that castings are likely to show pinholes.

There is also greater difficulty in annealing—usually it requires 200 or 300 degrees Fahrenheit higher temperature. This method may be safely used only when the property of bending, rather than strength, is required. Pipe fittings form a large part of the production of the cupola method. However, it makes a convenient melting medium for the production of anealing boxes.

Fig. 160. Section of Roof of Air Furnace

Air-Furnace Melting. The number of furnaces of this type far exceeds all others. In the issue of the *Foundry Magazine* for February, 1910, the number of the different types of furnaces engaged in the production of malleable in America was given as follows: air furnaces, 369; cupolas, 42; open-hearth furnaces, 21.

Figs. 158 and 159 show two general types of air furnace. In the furnace represented in Fig. 159 the bath is immediately behind the bridge, while that shown in Fig. 158 has its bath at the end, remote from the bridge.

Fuel is placed on the gate through the charging door D, which is of cast iron lined with fire brick. The hearth H is where the metal is placed when charged. E is the stack through which the gases finally escape. B is the bath where the molten metal collects and at its lowest point the tapping hole is located. The metal is charged by

Fig. 161. Complete Installation of Air Furnace

removing a part of the roof as shown at O, a section of which is shown in Fig. 160. Peepholes are shown at PPP, which are for observation.

Fig. 162. View Showing Method of Firing Air Furnace

The iron is charged on the hearth so as to leave openings between the pieces, and the molten metal should be skimmed from time to time so that it may receive the direct action of the burning gases passing over it.

Fig. 161 shows a type of air furnace complete. Fig. 162 is a view of the opposite side with a melter in the act of firing. Fig. 163 shows the slag hole, and the slag just skimmed off.

The air furnace requires greater skill to operate than does the cupola, and the fuel ratio is higher, but, if of good quality and

Fig. 163. Slag Hole

properly fired, is not excessive and should average about 3 of metal to 1 of fuel.

Open-Hearth Melting. It is said the open-hearth installation represents the highest type of melting yet devised, but the high first cost, combined with frequent and heavy repairs and skill required to operate, confine its use to the largest plants, and as long as the trade is satisfied with the quality of the product of the more easily operated air furnace, it is quite doubtful if the open hearth will be generally adopted. The description of the open-hearth furnace which has been given in Steel-Casting Practice may be referred to.

Iron Mixture. Without the proper mixture of iron no furnace will produce satisfactory iron, hence the importance of using the greatest care in this part of malleable practice.

That the reader may clearly understand the basic principles involved, it is necessary first to discuss the various materials entering into the mixture. These include pig iron, sprues, faulty castings, annealed scrap, steel scrap, and ferro-alloys

Good Composition. As all the materials have a bearing on the finished casting and should only be used as they affect this, it is at this time well to give an analysis for good malleable castings, which is as follows:

Element	Proportion (per cent)
Silicon	0.75 to 1.25
Carbon	3.00
Sulphur	0.04 (extreme)
Manganese	0.60 (extreme)
Phosphorus	0.20 (extreme)

There is considerable latitude allowed due to the class of work to be produced. Makers of heavy castings exclusively may specify their silicon from 0.75 to 1.50 per cent, while for very light work silicon from 1.25 to 2.00 per cent may be the rule. Total carbon should never run below 2.75 per cent in the hard, i.e., before the annealing. Manganese should average about 0.40, not much lower, and never above 0.60. Sulphur should always be as low as possible, 0.07 per cent being the high limit in the casting, hence the necessity for choosing irons for the mixture which will insure this. Phosphorus below 0.225 per cent is desired.

Pig Iron. Formerly it was thought that only charcoal pig was suitable for malleable practice, but today, owing to improved blast-furnace practice, coke irons which are known to the trade as *coke malleable* give first-rate results and are used to a considerable extent, yet it is seldom that the writer has heard of a mixture that did not include one or more of the well-known brands of charcoal iron known to the trade as *Mabel, Briar Hill, Hinckley,* and *Ella.* It is generally conceded that a mixture containing several brands of iron, or at least two or three grades of the same brand, produces better castings.

Scrap. The next problem which presents itself is the disposition of gates, sprues, and discards, which are daily accumulated in the works, and the per cent of which varies with the class of work produced, running as high as 60 per cent in the lightest work or not exceeding 25 per cent for very heavy castings. From this it will be seen that it is quite likely to be a varying element. The practice of taking the silicon content for every heat before castings go into the annealing operation gives opportunity for fairly exact calculations. Corrections may be made in the mixtures as may be found necessary, otherwise, should there be an accumulation of such material, it would soon become an unknown quantity and so be a source of annoyance as well as of loss to the management.

The annealed scrap offers more difficulties owing to the effect which even small amounts have on the quality of the product. Quite frequently there is no attempt to use this in the regular mixture but rather to utilize it in the production of annealing pots of which more will be said later.

The use of steel scrap in malleable mixtures is proving beneficial although the amount is at present limited to something like 10 per cent. This material should not be charged with the regular mixture, but should be introduced into the bath of molten metal so that it may be quickly covered by the protecting slag, for the steel must not be allowed to burn as this would seriously injure the quality of the castings.

It is also possible to use small amounts of gray-iron scrap, though it is seldom necessary to do so, and usually 5 per cent is the limit

Ferrosilicon. This material is carried in stock, either as a 0 50 or 0.75 per cent alloy for use in the ladle, or as a 14 to 20 per cent pig for use in the furnace

In choosing metals for the heat it first is necessary to ascertain the silicon content desired in the castings, and then to select such amounts of the different brands of pig iron at hand as are required to bring about the desired result, first making careful calculation of the amount of scrap to be cared for and its effect on the mixture as regards its silicon content. The previous section on Melting may be referred to regarding gray-iron mixture.

In conclusion, it would be well for the reader to clearly understand that it requires greater skill to produce malleables, and for this reason a well-equipped laboratory and a good metallurgist are almost necessities where high quality is the order of the day.

Malleable Casting

Variation from Gray=Iron Practice. The furnace having been duly charged for the day's melt with the desired mixture of metal, we will now consider the casting operation which differs only from gray-iron practice in that the metal contains a larger per cent of carbon in the combined form, melts at a lower temperature, and also cools more quickly in the ladle, and for this reason must be handled more rapidly. The hand ladles are of somewhat smaller capacity, usually about 25 pounds, as compared with 40 to 60 pounds in gray-iron practice

Carrying. This lighter burden allows the molder greater freedom in his movements. It is common practice to see the molder catching-in to the stream of molten metal and running to his floor that the molds may receive the benefit of the hottest metal possible. While this is possible in malleable-iron work, with the larger ladles of gray-iron practice, this would not only be exhausting, but highly dangerous as well

It must be remembered that the majority of work is light and that the floor space required for the setting-up of sufficient molds to pour, say, a 30-ton heat, is considerable, and even with the furnace located as it should be in the center of the works, there must be long carries. These are in part overcome by the installation of some overhead trolley system using 500-pound ladles; and where the nature of the work permits—i e., it is not too light—this method is of course preferable.

Cooling. As there is great danger of the castings developing cracks if exposed to the air while still red hot, it is far better practice to let them remain in the sand until they are at least black hot when they may be safely shaken out: the exception being some special work, as brake wheels, for example, in which there are developed great casting strains. In this case it is found best to shake out while still red hot and quickly place them in a so-called reheating oven which is already fired very hot. This furnace, after being fully charged with the day's output of this special work, is closed and the fire allowed to die out over night, when the castings will be found to be partly annealed, though not in a malleable sense. This treatment is found of considerable value in certain classes of work which otherwise might be hard to save.

Cleaning Castings. The castings having become cool so that they may be readily handled, a rough separation of castings and gates should be undertaken and the cores removed as far as possible, after which the castings should be inspected and all missruns or otherwise defective castings removed. The discards along with the gates and sprues should then be tumbled to remove the sand scale before being returned for remelting, otherwise it would form an excessive slag and require a larger amount of fuel to remelt.

Fig. 164. Modern Exhaust Tumbling Barrel

Hard-Rolling. After this rough sorting the castings are ready for the hard-rolling room which contains a series of tumbling barrels, all of which should be equipped with an exhaust system, or else the dust created in this department will become the bane of the plant. Fig. 164 shows an installation of modern exhaust tumbling barrels.

The castings should be rolled only long enough for the removal of the sand scale, usually accomplished in from 20 to 30 minutes. Some classes of work may be so delicate that it would be impossible to clean them in this manner without too great a loss from breakage, and in such cases the acid bath may be resorted to, or perhaps the sand blast which is fast superseding other methods of cleaning all classes of castings. Fig. 165 shows a New Haven sand-blast tumbling barrel which is well adapted to this work.

After this hard-rolling process the castings are removed to the trimming room where the gates and fins remaining may be easily removed with a hammer, thus saving much time in the grinding room after the annealing.

Annealing. We now arrive at one of the most important departments of the plant. No matter how carefully all previous operations may have been conducted, all will have been in vain should any

Fig. 165. Sand-Blast Tumbling Barrel

neglect creep into this part of the practice, for it is here that the very nature of the casting is changed from its hard and brittle state showing a white fracture, to the so-called black-heart malleable, the fracture showing a steely rim with a black velvety core.

This change is brought about by gradually bringing the temperature in the annealing ovens up to about 1600 degrees Fahrenheit, and by maintaining that temperature from 3 to 4 days, after which the fire is allowed to slowly die down; this whole process requires from 8 to 10 days. There have been attempts made to shorten this annealing process, usually by increasing the temperature some 200 degrees, thereby reducing the total period of the process to about 6

Fig. 166. Packing Annealing Boxes

Fig. 167. Hand Charging Truck

days; but this has been done at the expense of quality, and the best results are obtained by the former method.

Preparation of Castings. After inspection in the trimming room, the castings are brought to the annealing room which has its floor space divided into two parts—the packing floor, and the ovens. There are usually two rows of ovens, one on each side of the building, and the clear space between is used for packing the pots and also for dumping them after the annealing. The floor of this is made of 1-inch iron plates.

The annealing boxes, or laggers, may be either square or round, or perhaps more generally oblong, and are first cast 1 inch thick. These pots are piled three or four high—the first one is placed on an iron stool—all joints being luted up with mud made by adding water to the burnt sand from the rolling room with perhaps the

Fig. 168. Interior View of Annealing Oven

addition of a little fire clay. The scale used for packing is cinder squeezed from muck balls where wrought iron is made. It was formerly the practice to spread this scale upon the floor and sprinkle it daily with a solution of sal ammoniac to rust it, but later-day practice has proven this unnecessary.

As the castings come into the annealing room the operator places a pot on the stool, shovels in some scale, carefully placing in a layer of castings in such manner that none comes in contact with the sides of the pot or no two castings touch each other, then more scale and more castings are added until the pot is filled, as shown in Fig. 166. On this another pot is placed and duly packed, this to be continued until the pots are piled as high as desired, after which all joints are sealed with mud making the whole pile more or less

Fig. 169. Oven Charged

Fig. 170. Ash Pit and Firing Doors

air-tight. After this has been accomplished, the pots are placed in the oven either by a hand or by a power charging machine, as illustrated in Fig. 167.

FOUNDRY WORK 165

Oven. The annealing oven is quite simple. The principle involved is the introduction of heat from some convenient point and its distribution in a uniform manner, and the introduction of as

Fig. 171. Final Sorting of Castings

Fig. 172. Shipping Room

little air as possible. The combustion space should be no larger than necessary, the draft regulation perfect, and the bottom of the oven underlaid by a series of flues which allow the gases to circulate before escaping into the stack, so there may be as little loss of heat as possible. Oil, gas, or coal may be used for fuel as best adapted to the locality.

Fig. 168 shows the interior of an oven, while Fig. 169 shows the boxes in place. Fig. 170 is a side view of an oven showing the firing doors and the ash pits. Having placed the full number of

Fig. 173. Recording Pyrometer
Courtesy of The Bristol Company, Waterbury, Connecticut

boxes in the oven, the front is closed and the ovens are fired. As before stated this operation requires from 6 to 10 days from the time the fire is started until the oven has cooled sufficiently to allow the removal of the boxes.

As the boxes are withdrawn from the oven and are taken to the floor of the annealing room, they are suspended from an overhead trolley, or by a crane, and the castings are removed by striking the boxes several sharp blows with a medium-weight sledge hammer, the castings and scale falling upon the floor. The castings are now picked from the scale and it will be noted that there is some tendency for the scale to adhere to them. This may be removed by the ordinary rolling barrels, after which any gates or fins remaining should be ground off. The amount of labor required for this operation depends upon how carefully the gates were moved while castings were in the hard. After a final inspection, the castings should be ready for shipment. Figs. 171 and 172 show the castings being sorted out and ready for shipment in the shipping room.

Pyrometer. The use of the pyrometer in connection with the annealing furnace is almost obligatory. Fig. 173 shows a standard type of recording pyrometer. The pyrometer equipment is often placed in the office of the head executive of a local plant; it is possible for him to plug into any two of his battery of annealing furnaces at any time during the day. Also, in the morning, there is recorded a true record of temperatures for the night before. As no operator knows whether his furnace is under observation or not, this system has the tendency to keep the men at all times alert.

Finishing. The amount of finish given the castings varies with local conditions and class of castings produced. There are some classes of work where, by the use of leather scraps in the soft-rolling room, the work is so carefully cleaned and polished that the castings may be tinned or nickeled and sometimes gold- or silver-plated, making very beautiful work in which great strength is combined with cheapness of production.

BRASS WORK
ALLOYS

Distinctions. Cast iron, cast steel, and malleable iron, which we have previously considered, are three forms of the same metal—iron. The difference in their physical characteristics is due solely to a variation in the proportions of certain elements or metaloids combined with the iron.

The metals to be dealt with in this section are termed *alloys*—that is, mixtures of two or more separate metals. The common alloys in use in the foundry, for casting various machine parts, are made from combinations of copper, tin, and zinc, and are called *brass,* or *bronze.*

Brass and Bronze. Although the term brass is held by some authorities to cover any of these combinations, the general classification accepts brass as an alloy of copper and zinc, and bronze as an alloy of copper and tin. In some sections the latter is spoken of as *composition*

Bronze has been used by man in all ages Centuries before the Christian Era the Egyptians employed it for making coin, armor, and weapons, as well as household utensils, and statuettes of their gods. Analyses of many of these ancient relics show the composition to be almost identical with the bronzes of the present day. Brass also was in use before the time of Christ, but unquestionably bronze was of earlier origin.

Metals. A short discussion of the separate metals will help in understanding the properties of their alloys

Copper. Copper has a red color; it is hard, ductile, and very tough. It melts at about 2000 degrees F.; but it is difficult to make castings of the pure metal. Copper does not rust as does iron, and is one of the best conductors of heat and electricity. For this reason it is largely used in sheet form as a sheathing metal, and in the form of wire or rods for electrical transmission Casting copper is put on the market in ingots of special form weighing from 18 to 25 pounds each.

Tin. Tin is a white lustrous metal, very malleable, but lacking tenacity. It may be reduced extremely thin by rolling, as is shown by tin foil. It melts at 450 degrees F When a bar of tin is bent it will give a crackling sound known as the cry, which at once distinguishes it from other metals such as solder, lead, etc., which have similar external appearance It is put on the market in pigs weighing about 30 pounds and also in bars of about 1 pound each Its cost is approximately $1\frac{1}{2}$ times that of copper and 5 times as much as zinc Tin may be cast unalloyed, and is sometimes used to run pattern letters or small duplicate patterns cast in zinc chill molds. The addition of $\frac{1}{3}$ to $\frac{1}{2}$ by weight of lead gives a cheaper metal, however, and one that will run equally well.

Tin mixed with copper gives greater fluidity, lower melting point, and greater strength, changing the color from red to bright yellow. Serviceable alloys may contain as high as 20 per cent of tin. This gives a metal of golden yellow color, very hard, tough, and difficult to work. With larger percentages of tin the color shades to gray, the metal is hard, brittle, and has little strength, and has no value for engineering purposes.

Zinc. Zinc has a bluish white color; it is hard, but weak and brittle. The fracture shows very large crystals of characteristic shape. It melts at about 700 degrees F., and shrinks but little in cooling. For this reason it may be used to cast directly for small metal patterns to form chills from which soft-metal castings may be made for duplicating these patterns. If exposed to the air at high temperatures, zinc will volatilize, that is, turn to a gas and burn. It burns with a bluish flame, and throws off clouds of dense white smoke. For this reason great care must be used to keep the air away from it as much as possible when being melted or mixed in an alloy, for, aside from the loss of metal, an oxide is formed in the mixture which impairs the quality of the alloy.

Zinc is known in commerce under two names: when rolled into sheets it is called *zinc;* when in ingot form for casting, it is called *spelter*. These ingots are flat, approximately 8 by 1 by 17 inches, and weigh about 30 pounds. In this form they may be easily broken in small pieces for convenience in charging.

Zinc may be added to copper in a very wide range of proportions, the alloy increasing in hardness and losing ductility with the increase in the proportion of zinc. The color changes from the red of the copper to a full yellow when $\frac{1}{3}$ zinc is used. Further additions of zinc change the color to red, yellow, violet, and gray. The alloys are serviceable up to 40 or 50 per cent of zinc.

When zinc is mixed with melted metal, considerable reaction or boiling takes place, which tends to make a more thorough mixture and to drive impurities to the surface. For this reason a small proportion of zinc—2 or 3 per cent—is often stirred into bronze mixtures after the pot is drawn.

Lead. Lead has a bluish white color, and considerable luster when freshly cut. It is malleable, soft, and tough, but very weak. It melts at about 600 degrees F.

Lead is not used by itself as an alloy with copper. A very small proportion may be added to the standard mixture for brass or bronze.

TABLE VI

Proportions of Mixtures

Use	Copper		Tin		Zinc		Lead	
	(per cent)	(ounce)	(per cent)	(ounce)	(per cent)	(ounce)	(per cent)	(ounce)
Gun metal—for bearings, very tough hard mixture	83	16	12	2½	2.5	½	2.5	½
Steam or valve metal—cuts freely, very tough, resists corrosion	85	16	7	1¼	5	¾	3	½
Composition metal—for general use on small machine parts	90	16	5	1	5	½		
Art bronze—rich color, runs fluid at comparatively low heat	90	16	6	1	3	½	1	¼
Common yellow brass—for general run of machine castings	66.5	16			33.5	8		
Brass—to machine easier than the above, for same purposes	66	16	33			8	1	½
Antifriction metal—for journal boxes	1.8	1	64.7	32	33.35	16	1	½
Mixture—for small patterns, runs well, shrinks little			66	2			34	1

It will cause them to run more fluidly in pouring, and be softer for machining. For this reason, lead is added to bearing mixtures to advantage. But it tends to deaden the color and reduce the conductivity of the metal for electrical purposes.

Mixtures. *General Proportions.* The percentages given in Table VI are for convenience in comparison and for figuring large heats. The beginner, however, will generally melt but 1 or 2 pigs of copper at one time. These he will weigh first, and then figure the other portions of his mixture from this weight. In this case a formula given in pounds and ounces is much simpler.

Variation. From what has been said, it is understood that it is possible to vary these mixtures to meet special conditions. To harden or toughen an alloy, increase the tin, to soften it, reduce the tin. The same is true with zinc, but it will require larger proportionate changes in this metal to effect similar results in the alloy.

Phosphorus. Phosphorus is not a metal, but is a very active chemical element manufactured from bone ash. It has such an

TABLE VII
Phosphor-Bronze Mixtures

Element	Proportions of Alloy			
	Hard		Tough	
	per cent	(pounds)	per cent	(pounds)
Copper	87.5	8¾	90	9
Tin	12.25	1¼	9.75	½
Phosphorus			.25	
Phosphor tin	0.25	½		½
Total	100	10	100	10

affinity for the oxygen of the air, that in its pure state it must be kept under water, because the slightest scratch would cause it to burn fiercely. It forms the principal substance used in making the heads of matches

As a rule it is never used in the foundry in its pure state. For the production of phosphor-bronze castings there are several combined forms of phosphorus on the market. The most convenient of these is known as *phosphor tin*, which is metallic tin carrying various fixed percentages of phosphorus, of which 5 per cent is one very common proportion. Knowing the amount of phosphorus carried by the tin, the exact proportion for the entire alloy may be readily calculated. This element should not be used in alloys containing zinc or lead.

Phosphorus acts as a flux, combining with any oxidized or burned impurities in the bath of metal and driving them to the top. It tends to make the tin crystalline in form, in which condition it unites more firmly with the copper. It apparently unites chemically with copper, making that metal harder. The proportion of phosphorus should not exceed 0.75 per cent, while 0.25 to 0.40 per cent are safer proportions.

Two typical mixtures, one using 5 per cent phosphor tin, are given in Table VII.

PRODUCTION

Molding Materials. Natural molding sands are used for brass work. They are usually finer than sands used in iron work, because brass parts are generally small and often have fine detail which must be brought out very sharply in the mold. For this reason, also, the sands should have more alumina or bond than iron sands. This increase of bond is possible because the metals entering the mold are not as hot as iron would be, and therefore do not require as much vent, but they have a greater tendency to cut the mold.

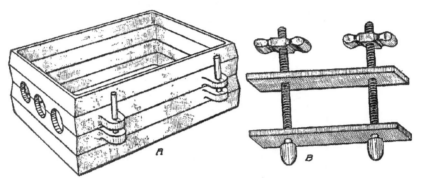

Fig. 174. *A*—Flask for Brass; *B*—Screw Clamp

For the general run of work the whole heap is kept in good condition by the frequent addition of new sand, but on large work a facing mixture is used similar to that of the iron foundry.

Burnt sand, powdered charcoal, and partainol are all good parting materials; the last two are best on small work, as they make a cleaner joint. Since they make a good facing for the mold, they are not blown off of the patterns.

Fig. 175. Spill Trough

Equipment. *Tools.* The brass molder uses practically the same kind of tools, such as shovels, sieves, rammers, and molder's tools generally, as already have been described.

Flasks. Snap flasks may be used, but the pins, hinges, and catches must be kept in careful adjustment so that the parts of the mold shall register perfectly. The same is true of the larger box flasks for floor work.

The most typical brass flasks are of cast iron with accurately fitting round steel pins, as seen in Fig. 174 at *A*. They have holes on the joint at one end of the flask so that the mold may be set upright when pouring. This gives a decided additional pouring pressure with a minimum thickness of sand over the castings.

Boards without cleats support the sand in the flask, and the whole is clamped, before setting on end, by means of some form of double-screw clamp similar to the illustration *B*, in Fig. 174.

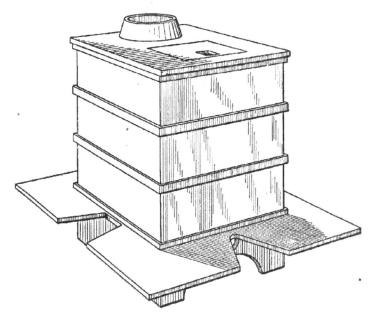

Fig. 176. Drying Stove

Spill Trough. Great care is taken in the brass shop to save all the shot and spilled metal possible. To this end, when the molds are to be poured on end, they are leaned against a cast-iron spill trough such as shown in Fig. 175. There should be a 1-inch layer of sand over the bottom of this tray. The crucible is held over it when pouring the molds, thus making it possible to conveniently catch any metal that is spilled.

Drying Stove. For thin work the face of the molds are skin-dried to drive off the moisture before the metal enters the mold. Drying stoves, similar to that shown in Fig. 176, are used for this purpose. When the mold is finished, the two halves are carefully sprayed with a weak molasses water, and the flask is set on end on the wide platform with the face of the mold next to the stove. When sufficiently dry, the mold is closed and poured at once.

Principles of Work. *Size of Heat.* Brass work deals, as a rule, with smaller quantities in every way than does iron work. The patterns are generally smaller, and the brass molder takes particular pride in making all his joints so neat that hardly a fin shows on his castings. The matter of catching the shot metal has been mentioned. Up to the time of the introduction of the oil-melting furnace, it was customary to heat a pot of metal for each molder. These heats were comparatively small, so that the molder would make up possibly 6 or 8 molds, then draw his pot and pour them, running in this way several heats in a day. Using the furnace, several heats are run each day, but a much larger quantity of metal is melted at each heat, so that the work of several molders is poured with exactly the same metal.

Molds. A mold for brass should be rammed about the same as for iron. On name plates and thin work, after the initial facing of sifted sand has been properly tucked with the fingers, the flask is filled heaping full of sand. Then by the aid of a rope hanging down from the ceiling, the molder springs up on top of the flask and packs the mold with his feet, the weight of his body giving the right degree of firmness to the sand. Stove-plate molders often pack their flasks in the same way.

The main differences between making up molds for brass and those for iron are due to the three following causes: brass melts at a lower heat; it does not run as fluid as iron; it has about double the shrinkage of iron. For these reasons the sand may be somewhat less porous and still vent sufficiently, if risers are placed to allow for the escape of the air. On bench work the vent wire is not used The runners for brass should be larger than for iron, and the gates, instead of being broad and shallow, should be more semicircular in section. Pouring molds on end gives the pressure necessary to force a more sluggish metal to take a sharp impression, and the heavy runners shown in the following examples serve to feed the casting as it shrinks. Forms of skimming gates, as explained in an earlier section, are used to good advantage when the work is of a very particular nature.

FOUNDRY WORK

Cores for brass work are made up as previously described. To give a smoother surface on the small cores, about $\frac{1}{3}$ molding sand is often mixed in with the beach sand of the stock mixture.

Examples of Work. To illustrate more clearly some of the typical methods of brass work, let our first example be a thin flat plate with decoration in low relief on one side.

Place the pattern face down, a little below the center of flask. Sift on facing through a No. 16 sieve, then tuck, fill, and pack, as previously described. Roll over and make a joint. Now cut a half section of the main runners and risers, but do not connect them with the mold at this stage. Dust on parting material from a bag, and ram the other half of the flask just hard enough to stand handling.

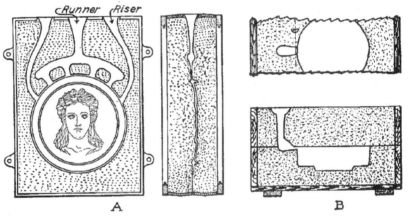

Fig. 177. A—Mold for Thin Plate; B—Mold for Heavy Plate

Separate the flask; spray the face of the mold with weak molasses water, and dust on it from a bag some finely powdered pumice stone, or any fine strong sand, and over this a little parting dust. Now replace this half over the pattern, and re-ram to the required firmness, and again separate and this time draw the pattern.

The impression of the runners and risers cut in the first half of the mold show as ridges on the second half packed, and serve as guides for cutting the runners to a full round section. Connect the gates in four places, as shown in A, Fig. 177. Skin-dry the mold and it is ready to close and pour.

Dusting fine sand on the face of the mold, then reprinting, as it is termed, ensures a very smooth, perfect mold face. Where the mold is not skin-dried, flour is dusted over the face, allowed to stand

TABLE VIII
Crucible Sizes

Number	Holding Capacity (Liquid Measure)			Measurements Outside				Capacity Weight of Water
				Height	Diameter			
					Top	Bilge	Bottom	
	(gallon)	(quart)	(pint)	(inches)	(inches)	(inches)	(inches)	(pounds)
0				2	$1\frac{1}{2}$	$1\frac{5}{8}$	$1\frac{1}{4}$	
0000				3	$2\frac{3}{8}$	$2\frac{1}{2}$	$1\frac{3}{4}$	
6		1		$6\frac{1}{2}$	$5\frac{1}{4}$	$5\frac{1}{8}$	$3\frac{3}{4}$	2.08
12		2		8	$6\frac{1}{4}$	$6\frac{3}{4}$	5	4.16
30	1	1	1	11	$8\frac{5}{8}$	$9\frac{1}{4}$	$6\frac{1}{4}$	11.5
60	3			14	$10\frac{3}{8}$	$11\frac{5}{8}$	8	25
90	4			$15\frac{7}{8}$	$11\frac{1}{2}$	$12\frac{1}{2}$	9	33.3
300	12	2		22	$16\frac{1}{4}$	$17\frac{1}{2}$	$12\frac{1}{2}$	104.

for a short time, and then blown off. This makes a good facing. Cutting the heavy runner over the top of the thin plate ensures a sufficient supply of clean hot metal to the gates under a large enough pressure to force the metal into every detail of the mold before it has time to chill.

In *B*, Fig. 177, is shown the difference in construction of the gate when a heavier piece is cast with the flask setting horizontally. The gate proper is cut in the drag, but a good feeding head is cut out of the cope side to keep the metal in the riser liquid until the casting has solidified.

Duplication. For duplicating work, the sand match, oil match, or follow board are used, the same as for iron work. Fig. 178 shows a typical set of castings run from the end and made from gated patterns set in an oil match. Steady pins are placed on the gates to facilitate a clean lift.

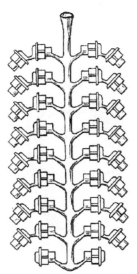

Fig. 178. Duplicated Gated Work

Melting. *Characteristics.* All alloy metals, and especially zinc and tin, burn if exposed to the air while melting. To prevent this burning the brass melter endeavors to so control the draft in his furnace that all oxygen entering the gates combines with the fuel, and that the gases which may reach the metal shall contain no free oxygen. For this reason, the ordinary brass furnace is a natural-draft furnace, although a forced draft is often connected below the grates to make combustion independent of atmospheric conditions.

The metal does not come in direct contact with the fuel, but is contained in fire-clay pots called crucibles, which are bedded in the fire. Hard coal or coke is used for fuel. These crucibles, Fig. 179, *A*, are manufactured from a very refractory fire-clay mixture, and are strong and tough, even at a high temperature. They are lifted in and out of the furnace by the tongs shown at *B*, Fig. 179. For the larger sizes a crane is used for hoisting the pot. Crucibles are classed by number, as seen in Table VIII. New crucibles should always be annealed before using, that is, brought very slowly to a low red heat.

Natural-Draft Furnace. Furnaces of this type are usually called brass furnaces, and may be bought on the market made up in single complete units. Fig. 180 illustrates one of a battery of several furnaces connecting with a common flue. The top is on a level with the molding floor. The sketch shows clearly the principles of construction. A cast-iron bottom plate *A*, with a circular opening, carries a shell of boiler plate lined with fire brick. The diameter inside the lining should be 6 inches larger than the crucible to be used. A top plate, with a similar opening, binds the whole together. On one side, below the top, the opening *B*, which may be formed by a cast-iron box, connects with the flue or stack. Two heavy ribs cast on the bottom plate rest on a pair of rails as shown, and these rails are supported by suitable piers of brickwork about 2 feet high, so that ashes may be conveniently removed when the furnace is dumped.

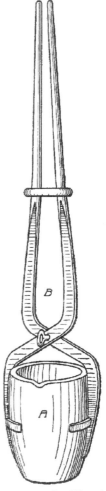

Fig. 179. Crucible and Tongs

In the space made by the ribs, between the bottom plate and the rails, the grate bars *C* are set. These bars are loose and may be pulled out when it is desired to dump the fire for the day.

Operation. Before starting the fire in preparing to run off a heat, a good plan is to use a half fire brick on which to rest the crucible, or the bottom of a worn-out crucible cut off to the height of 4 inches or 5 inches may be turned upside down and used for this purpose.

Sufficient time and special care should be exercised in placing the metal in a crucible. It is more or less dangerous to jam in the charges, so particular care should be taken to see that they are placed

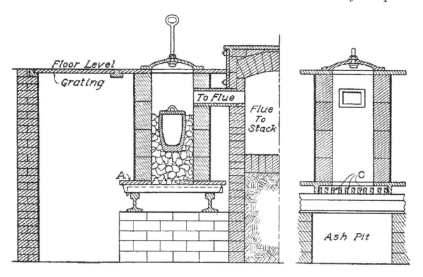

Fig. 180. Natural-Draft Furnace

in the crucible loosely. Graphite is the crucible's principal ingredient; the only expansion possible to a crucible comes from its clay body, hence, if the charges are wedged in a crucible and jammed to fit tight, their expansion, which is much greater than the expansion of the crucible, cracks the latter before the melting point is reached. The crucible should be kept covered, especially for brass.

In melting brass, melt down the copper first, then the scrap. When this is melted, charge the zinc and stir well before lifting the pot. Allow the mixture to come to the proper heat again, then pull the pot, skim off the dross, and stir in the lead if any is called for, just before pouring. In bronze the same method is pursued, but both the tin and zinc are stirred in after the pot is drawn. In mixing in the zinc in brass, care must be taken to plunge it well under the surface

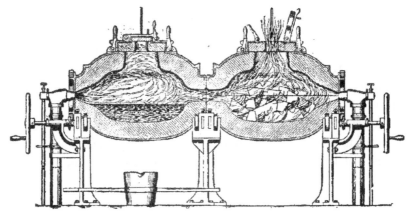

Fig. 181. Section through Oil Furnace

of the copper with long handled pick-up tongs, and to hold the piece down with the stirring bar until it has melted.

Where a large casting requires more metal than can be melted in a single crucible, several furnaces must be used and the contents of their various crucibles assembled into one large pouring ladle just before pouring.

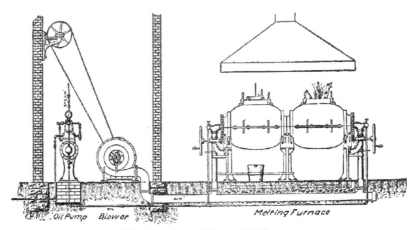

Fig. 182. General Views of Oil Furnace

Gas or Oil Furnace. With the development of natural-gas and crude-oil burners for commercial heating, several good furnaces have been designed in which a large quantity of metal can be melted at one time. Fig. 181 shows a furnace of this character in section. This type has tandem melting chambers with burners at the end, which may be used separately or both together. The waste gases from the

Fig. 183. Sprue Trimmer
Courtesy of Toledo Machine and Tool Company, Toledo, Ohio

bath of liquid metal are used to heat up a fresh charge in the other chamber. The metal is charged and poured from the openings at the top of the furnace. Each chamber may be revolved separately, to empty the furnace when the charge is melted. Fig. 182 shows the general arrangement of the oil feed pump and blower for these melting furnaces. The flame plays directly on to the metal. The oil pressure should remain constant at about 5 pounds per square inch. But the air pressure is regulated to vary the intensity of the heat as desired.

Fig. 184. Dipping Basket

The pouring ladle must be well heated before using. This is done with a special gas burner, or, when crucibles are used, they are often heated by means of a small fire in an ordinary furnace.

Different sizes of furnaces are built to melt from 250 to 2000 pounds of metal at a heat. Twelve or fourteen heats a day can be run. The saving is approximately 50 per cent in time, and is also very considerable in expense, over ordinary crucible furnaces of equal capacity.

Cleaning. When the castings are taken from the sand they should be rapped smartly to free all loose sand, then, if machining is to be done on them, they should be plunged, while hot, into water. This softens the castings. This method is used also to blow out cores from small work.

Fig. 185. Magnetic Separator

Since brass does not burn into the sand as much as iron, the small castings in many shops are brushed clean, before being cut from the gates, by means of a circular scratch brush mounted on a spindle similar to a polishing wheel.

A sprue-trimmer, shown in Fig. 183, is part of the equipment of a brass foundry. These machines are made to operate by foot as shown, or by power. With them the castings are cut neatly and quickly from the runners.

Pickling. A good method of cleaning brass and bronze is by pickling. Make a mixture of 2 parts common nitric acid and 1 part sulphuric acid, in a stone jar. Place the piece to be cleaned in a stone dipping basket, Fig. 184, and dip once into the acid, then wash off in clean water, and dry in sawdust.

Chip Separation. In many cases, brass chips and filings are turned back to the foundry to be remelted. The smallest portions of steel or iron in these would prevent their being used in this way, as they make extremely hard spots in the castings.

Fig. 185 shows a magnetic separator which effectively removes all steel and iron chips. The brass chips and sweepings from the machine shop are placed in the hopper of this machine. They are caused to be spread out on one side of a slowly revolving brass covered drum. Inside of this brass shell are strong magnets which hold to their surfaces the steel and iron chips, while the brass chips drop off into a tote box. A stiff brush at the back of the cylinder removes the iron chips, and they drop into a separate box.

SHOP MANAGEMENT

PLANT ARRANGEMENT

Governing Factors. The success of a foundry depends upon the ability of its managers to promptly turn out castings which meet the requirements demanded of them, at the lowest possible cost commensurate with the quality of the work. In this article we wish to direct the attention of students to some features in the way of equipment and management which aid in accomplishing these results.

The most important processes in the foundry are the following: melting metal, making molds, and pouring them. Much of the work necessary in preparing for these processes consists in handling heavy materials such as coke, iron, sand, etc. To reduce this handling to its lowest limits, as to distances, number of re-handlings, and methods of conveyance, are problems to be considered in the plan of the shop as a whole.

TYPICAL FOUNDRY

General Plan. To briefly illustrate some of the points to be brought out, let us consider the plan of the shop shown in Fig. 186, and its sectional elevation shown in Fig. 187.

FOUNDRY WORK

Building. The building is of steel construction, and the columns supporting the roof trusses serve also to carry the tracks for the overhead traveling cranes.

The outer walls should be filled in with some good weather-resisting material, of which there is nothing better than brick. These walls should be of good height and have a sufficient window area to supply light well in toward the middle of the shop.

Ventilation. The method of heating and ventilating best adapted for a foundry is the indirect fan system. One or more large

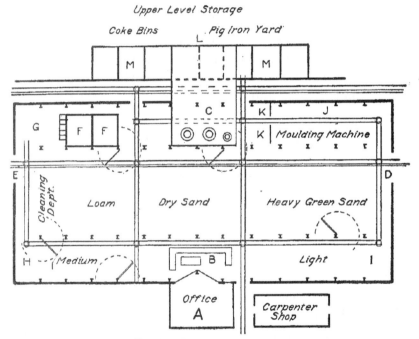

Fig. 186. Typical Plan of Foundry

fans, situated generally toward the ends of the shop, draw fresh air in through a compact system of steam coils, and, by means of overhead piping, deliver it to all portions of the shop. The impure gases are carried off through ventilators in the clearstory at the top of the roof.

Floor. The floor of the foundry should consist of molding sand, the depth of the sand floor varying with the class of work to be done. If the natural soil of the grounds is open and porous, a thickness of 3 or 4 inches of clay, well rolled down, should be put in underneath the sand floor. This will help greatly in keeping the molding floor in good condition, as it prevents the moisture draining out of the sand.

Shop Office. The foundry office should be located at such a point that the foreman can command a view of the whole shop. It should be convenient to the different departments and at the same time be protected as far as possible from dust. The office room, shown in Fig. 186 at A, is built on the outside of the main building, but has a large bay window which projects a few feet into the shop from which all corners of the foundry can be seen.

Pattern Room. A space B, having suitable low tables and shelving, is reserved near the office for the temporary storing of patterns in daily use. This brings them directly under the attention of the foreman and his assistants who can readily check the patterns as they come in and quickly find those requiring prompt attention.

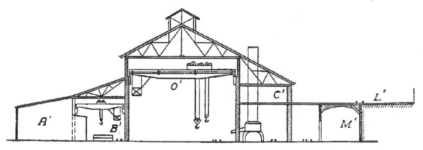

Fig. 187. Typical Elevation of Foundry

Cupolas. At C are shown the cupolas, directly opposite the foreman's office, and so situated that all of the molding floors may be served as quickly as possible without interfering one with the other.

In large foundries there are two or more cupolas, to admit of different mixtures being melted simultaneously. Often a comparatively small cupola is installed near the floor for light work for the service of that floor alone.

The blowers should be placed near the cupolas, avoiding long connecting wind pipes. The application of electric motors removes the necessity of concentrating the power at one point in the shop.

Molding Divisions. *Heavy Work.* The main bay of the foundry is devoted to the heaviest work and is served by at least two overhead cranes.

FOUNDRY WORK

The heavy green-sand castings are made at one end so that the flasks for this work may be stored in yards near by and be brought in through the door D. These molds are made up farthest from the cleaning shed, because only the castings themselves need be transferred there.

The flasks and rigging for the dry-sand and loam molds should be brought in through the opposite door E. The loam work, as a rule, is the most bulky to handle and should be nearest the cleaning

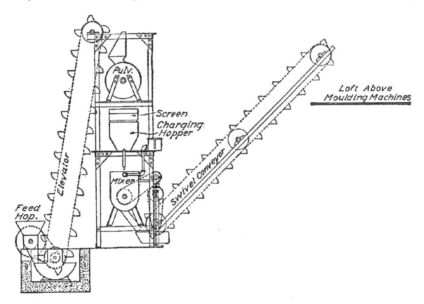

Fig. 188. Automatic Sand Mixer

sheds so that it need not be carried across the other floors. Both dry-sand and loam floors are convenient to the large ovens F.

Core Shop. The core shop is situated in the side bay at G, to make it convenient to swing the large cores on to the buggies to be run into the large ovens. A jib crane near the corner of these ovens makes the men working on such cores independent of the traveling crane. The ovens for small cores are built along the side of the large ovens and utilize the same stoke hole, ash pit, and stack.

Light Work. Distributed through the side bays also are the medium-work floor H, the light-work floor I, and the molding-machine floor J. This ensures a supply of good light necessary to the smaller details of this class of work.

Machines. The molding machines are placed on that side of the shop near the sand storage sheds, to allow for handling the sand by means of belt conveyors with hoppers above the machines, an illustration of which is shown in Fig. 188.

The sand-mixing space is in the side bay near the cupolas at K, and is furnished with power from independent motors or from a jack shaft leading from the blower room. This position affords direct access to the sand bins The raw material after being mixed and tempered is delivered by barrow or sand car direct to the various floors. The mixers might be installed in one of the storage vaults across the roadway.

Materials. *Unloading.* The quickest means of unloading either wagon or carload lots of material is by dumping, where the material can be so handled. One of two things is necessary to accomplish this: either the storage bins must be placed in a basement underneath the roadbed; or the roadway must be run up an incline over the top of the bins. The former method is more frequently met with in the crowded condition of the large cities, but the latter is preferable because less time is consumed in running material up an incline in large quantities than is required to hoist small quantities more frequently from a basement.

Storage. At L and L', Figs. 186 and 187, are shown the storage yards for pig iron and coke; these are on a level with the charging platform of the cupola, C and C', and the materials can be loaded on cars and pushed directly to the charging door. In some modern shops these push cars are built so that their load may be dumped as a whole into the cupola.

The storage for core-oven fuel, sands, and clay, is shown at MM, in bins built underneath the tracks and on a level with the foundry floor. These bins should be arranged to open on top, with a chute under the track and a trap at the side, so that coal or sand may either be dumped or shoveled directly into them.

Handling Systems. *Tracks.* In the largest shops a standard-gage track should run directly through the main foundry, and there should be also similar tracks through the roadway next the cupola bay for convenience in removing the dump. The track over the storage bins has been mentioned.

Two methods of transferring material between departments within the shop, aside from the cranes, are the overhead-trolley

FOUNDRY WORK

system, Fig. 189, and the narrow-gage industrial railway. The former is of advantage in manufacturing plants where the loads to be transferred are nearly uniform in weight and frequency of handling. This system leaves gangways smooth and free from obstructions. For general work, however, the industrial railways are more frequently installed. These serve all floors to deliver flasks, sand, or iron, and to remove castings.

Cranes. Of the many styles of overhead traveling cranes that are on the market, those using electricity as the motive power are undoubtedly the most serviceable. The cranes in the main foundry indicated at O', Fig. 187, should have two hoisting drums on the carriage; one for such light work as handling flasks, rigging, and patterns; the other for the heavy work on the large ladles and castings.

Fig. 189. Overhead Track and Trolley

Small jib cranes furnished with a 2- to 4-ton air or electric hoist placed on the side of a man's floor make it possible for the molder and helper to handle work of considerable size by themselves, and prevent loss of time from waiting for the overhead crane.

The method of distributing the melted metal varies with the class of work made. In shops doing general jobbing work, the ladles for pouring the largest work are carried from the cupola directly by the overhead cranes.

Bay Floor. For serving the floors in the bays one of the systems mentioned above is generally used. The metal is conveyed to the floor in a large ladle and from this smaller ones are filled and carried by hand or by a small crane to the molds.

Cleaning Department. The cleaning department should be situated at one end of the shop near E, Fig. 186, or in a shed extension to the foundry proper. It requires space to pile the castings as they are brought from the floors with sufficient room for the men to begin work on these piles. As a rule, the smaller castings are first collected and put through the tumbling barrels, then the medium work is cleaned by hand or by sand blast, this leaves room for work around the largest pieces. As soon as castings are cleaned they are weighed and shipped to the customer, store house, or to the department which does the next operation upon them.

PERFORMANCE
LABOR

Division. The division of labor in a foundry is briefly as follows:

Superintendent. The superintendent is responsible for the operation of the foundry as a whole. He hires the men and oversees the purchase of materials and supplies, having under him clerks who keep track of the details of this work. Some of the things to which he gives personal attention are: In consultation with his foreman he gives personal attention to the receipt of the most important patterns, decides how they shall be molded; on what floor and with what mixture they shall be poured. He devises ways and means of increasing the productiveness of his shop.

Foreman. The foreman or his assistants must be in the shop a sufficient time before work begins for the day to see that each molder has work laid out for him, and must keep the men supplied with work through the day. He estimates the amount of the charge for the day and directs the melter as to mixtures

It is the duty of the foreman and his assistants to give directions to the apprentice boys and to see that these directions are carried out to the best of the boys' ability.

Molders. The molders should give their entire time to making up molds. On floor work they are usually given a helper who carries flasks, cores, chaplets, etc., and does the heavier work when handling the sand. When the molds are poured and his flasks stripped off the molder is through for the day.

Laborers. Most modern shops employ a night gang of laborers to put the shop in proper shape for the molders to start their special work immediately when the whistle blows in the morning These men remove the castings from the sand and transfer them to the cleaning shed. They pick out all bars and gaggers used in the molds and stow them in place. They temper and cut the sand and dig any pits necessary for bedding in work.

SAFETY FIRST

Accident Prevention. While it may be an impossibility to wholly prevent accidents in and about the foundry, much has been accomplished in that line. Mechanical safeguards are now in pretty general use in modern foundries. It is only the out-of-date shop which is conspicuous for neglect in providing them.

Personal Factor. Only some of the more important items regarding safety are called to the reader's attention, and perhaps the most important one of all is to teach the workman to think *safety first*. As an example, in a foundry employing 850 men there were, during a period of 6 months, 57 accidents involving loss of time. Not one of these was due to the lack of mechanical safeguards; all were results of carelessness on the part of the injured, or of negligence by their fellow workmen.

Clothing. A large percentage of accidents in the foundry are in the nature of burns from hot metal, and again by far the greater part of these are below the knee. This shows the practical necessity for a legging of some material which would resist the hot metal. All emp'oyes in the foundry who come in contact in any manner with the work of pouring, or of shaking out flasks after pouring, when the hot sand may be just as dangerous as the molten metal, should be compelled to wear the foundry or congress shoe.

Shop Equipment. There should be frequent inspection of all foundry rigging, such as crane hooks, chains, and ladle shanks, also great care should be used under the cupola and tapping spout, as any excess of moisture, were molten metal to be spilled upon it, would cause explosions and probably seriously injure someone.

In the cleaning room, protection for the eyes from flying chips of metal is important; so, also, are guards over grinding wheels which should be equipped with an efficient exhaust to care for dust.

While there are many more things which might be mentioned regarding safety, as applied to foundry practice, those already mentioned should be sufficient to cause the student to *think* safety, to put his thoughts in practice and to teach others to do likewise.

PHYSICAL RESULTS

Checking. The methods of mixing iron by analysis have been previously dealt with, but these mixtures must be checked by physical tests on the resulting castings. Two systems of checking are now in more or less general use throughout the United States.

Keep's Mechanical Analysis. A very complete system of regulating mixtures, termed by the inventor *Mechanical Analysis* has been devised by W. J. Keep, of Detroit, Michigan, who has had long experience in this subject. In Fig. 190, *A* shows a follow board arranged with patterns and yokes. The test bars are ½ inch square and 12 inches long. They are cast in green sand with their ends chilled against the faces of the cast-iron yokes, shown in the cut. Three molds should be cast each heat, and the test bars allowed to cool in the molds.

Silicon and Shrinkage. The analysis is based on the fact that silicon is the most important variable chemical element in cast iron,

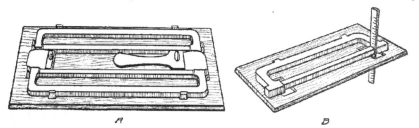

Fig. 190. *A*—Keep's Test-Bar Pattern; *B*—Measuring Shrinkage

and that shrinkage in castings is inversely proportionate to the silicon in the mixture.

The first test, as shown at *B*, Fig. 190, is to replace each bar in the same yoke in which it was cast and by means of a specially graduated taper scale to ascertain accurately the amount of shrinkage.

The shrinkage of the bars when the castings prove satisfactory, should be considered the standard for that class of work for that shop. If at any time the shrinkage is greater than the standard, increase the silicon by using more soft pig; if it is less, decrease silicon by using more scrap or cheaper iron.

Chilled Depth. The depth of chill on the castings is measured after chipping off a piece from the end of the bar.

Transverse Strength. The third test is to obtain the transverse strength of each bar. This is done on a special testing machine

FOUNDRY WORK

which gives a graphical record of the deflection and the ultimate breaking load. These dead loads will vary with different mixtures approximately from 340 to 500 pounds.

Deductions. Quoting from Mr. Keep's circular:

With high shrinkage and high strength of a ½-inch square test bar, heavy castings will be strong but small castings may be brittle.

With low shrinkage and high strength, large castings will be weak and small castings will be strong.

With uniform shrinkage, an increase in the strength of a ½-inch square test bar will increase the strength of all castings proportionately.

Arbitration=Bar Tests. The other form of tests was devised by a committee of the American Foundrymen's Association, and is recommended in the Proposed Standard Specifications for Gray-Iron Castings by the American Society for Testing Materials.

Test Bar. The test bar specified is $1\frac{1}{4}$ inches in diameter and 15 inches long, and is known as the *arbitration bar*.

The tensile test is not recommended, but, if called for, a special threaded test piece is turned down from the arbitration bar, and has a test section 0.8 inch in diameter and 1 inch between shoulders.

The transverse test is made with supports 12 inches apart.

Fig. 191 shows a sketch of the patterns for these bars. Two bars are rammed in a flask and poured on end. The small prints on the two bar patterns project into the cope and are connected by one pouring basin. A special green-sand mixture is specified for making these molds; the molds are to be baked before pouring, and the bars allowed to remain in the sand until cold.

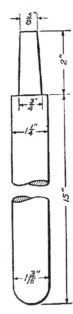

Fig. 191. Pattern for Arbitration Bar

Specifications. Table IX shows the specified requirements; in this connection castings are distinguished as follows:

Unless furnace iron is specified, all gray castings are understood to be made by the cupola process.

Light castings are those having any section less than ½ inch.

Heavy castings have no section less than 2 inches.

Medium castings are those not included in the above.

TABLE IX
Arbitration=Bar Standards

Grade of Castings	Chemical Properties	Physical Properties	
	Sulphur Content High Limit (per cent)	Transverse Test* Minimum Load (lb.)	Tensile Strength Low Limit (lb per sq in)
Light	0.08	2500	18,000
Medium	0.10	2900	21,000
Heavy	0.12	3300	24,000

PRACTICAL DATA

Using Percentage

(1) To find the percentage of any number when the **rate per cent** is given: Multiply the number by the rate per cent and set the decimal point two places to the left.

Example: Find 7.5 per cent of 35. 35×7.5 = 262.5; decimal point moved two places to the left gives   Ans. 2.625

(2) To find what rate per cent one number is of another: Add two ciphers to the percentage and divide by the number on which the percentage is reckoned.

Example: What per cent of 75 tons is 9 tons? 900÷75 = 12.
     Ans. 12 per cent

(3) To find a number when the rate per cent and the percentage are known: Add two ciphers to the percentage and divide by the rate per cent.

Example: If 68 pounds is 15 per cent of the entire charge, how many pounds in the total charge? Ans. 6800÷15 = 453.33 pounds

(4) To find what number is a certain per cent more or less than a given number: (*a*) When the given number is more than the required number, add two ciphers to the number and divide by 100 plus the rate per cent.

Example: 465 is 35 per cent more than what number?
     Ans. 46500÷(100+35)135 = 344.4

(*b*) When the given number is less than the required number add two ciphers to the number and divide by 100 minus the rate per cent.

---

*In no case, shall the deflection be under 0.10 of an inch.

FOUNDRY WORK

Storage Data
Square Box Measure

Size (inches)	Capacity
24 × 16 × 28	1 barrel
16 × 16¾ × 8	1 bushel
8¼ × 8¼ × 4	1 gallon
4 × 4¼ × 4	1 quart

Molding Material Weights

Material	Amount (cu. ft.)	Weight (ton)
River sand	21	1
Pit sand	22	1
Stiff clay	28	1

Example. 526 is 23 per cent less than what number?
   Ans. $52600 \div (100-23) = 52600 \div 77 = 683.116$

Mensuration

Circumference of a circle	= diameter × 3.1416
Area of a square or rectangle	= base side × height
Area of a triangle	= base × ½ × perpendicular height
Area of a circle	= diameter squared × .7854
Convex surface of a cylinder	= circumference × height
Convex surface of a sphere	= circumference × diameter
Contents of a rectangular solid	= area of base × height
Contents of a cylinder	= area of base circle × height
Contents of a sphere	= cube of diameter × .5236
One side of square having same area as given circle	= diameter × .8862 or circumference × .2821

Conversion Factors

Inches	×	0.08333	= feet
Square inches	×	0.00695	= sq. feet
Cubic inches	×	0.00058	= cu. feet
Cubic inches	×	0.004329	= U. S. gallons
Cubic feet	×	1728	= cu. inches
Cubic yards	×	27	= cu. feet
U. S. gallons of water	×	8.33	= pounds
U. S. gallons of water	×	231.00	= cu. inches
Pounds of water	×	27.72	= cu. inches
Ounces of water	×	1.735	= cu. inches

Circular Areas and Circumferences

Diameter	Area	Circumference	Diameter	Area	Circumference	Diameter	Area	Circumference	Diameter	Area	Circumference
1/8	0.0123	.3926	10	78.54	31.41	30	706.86	94.24	65	3318.3	204.2
1/4	0.0491	.7854	1/2	86.59	32.98	31	754.76	97.38	66	3421.2	207.3
3/8	0.1104	1.178	11	95.03	34.55	32	804.24	100.5	67	3525.6	210.4
1/2	0.1963	1.570	1/2	103.86	36.12	33	855.30	103.6	68	3631.6	213.6
5/8	0.3067	1.963	12	113.09	37.69	34	907.92	106.8	69	3739.2	216.7
3/4	0.4417	2.356	1/2	122.71	39.27	35	962.11	109.9	70	3848.4	219.9
7/8	0.6013	2.748	13	132.73	40.85	36	1017.8	113.0	71	3959.2	223.0
1	0.7854	3.141	1/2	143.13	42.41	37	1075.2	116.2	72	4071.5	226.1
1/8	0.9940	3.534	14	153.93	43.98	38	1134.1	119.3	73	4185.3	229.3
1/4	1.227	3.927	1/2	165.13	45.55	39	1194.5	122.5	74	4300.8	232.4
3/8	1.484	4.319	15	176.71	47.12	40	1256.6	125.6	75	4417.8	235.6
1/2	1.767	4.713	1/2	188.69	48.69	41	1320.2	128.8	76	4536.4	238.7
5/8	2.078	5.105	16	201.06	50.26	42	1385.4	131.9	77	4656.0	241.9
3/4	2.405	5.497	1/2	213.82	51.83	43	1452.2	135.0	78	4778.3	245.0
7/8	2.761	5.890	17	226.98	53.40	44	1520.5	138.2	79	4901.6	248.1
2	3.141	6.283	1/2	240.52	54.97	45	1590.4	141.3	80	5026.5	251.3
1/8	3.976	7.068	18	254.46	56.54	46	1661.9	144.5	81	5153.0	254.4
1/4	4.908	7.854	1/2	268.80	58.11	47	1734.9	147.6	82	5281.0	257.6
3/8	5.989	8.639	19	283.52	59.69	48	1809.5	150.7	83	5410.6	260.7
3	7.068	9.424	1/4	298.64	61.26	49	1885.7	153.9	84	5541.7	263.8
1/4	8.295	10.21	20	314.16	62.83	50	1963.5	157.0	85	5674.5	267.0
1/2	9.621	10.99	1/2	330.06	64.40	51	2042.8	160.2	86	5808.8	270.1
3/4	11.044	11.78	21	346.36	65.97	52	2123.7	163.3	87	5944.6	273.3
4	12.566	12.56	1/2	363.05	67.54	53	2206.1	166.5	88	6082.1	276.4
1/2	15.904	14.13	22	380.13	69.11	54	2290.2	169.6	89	6221.1	279.6
5	19.635	15.70	1/2	397.60	70.68	55	2375.8	172.7	90	6361.7	282.7
1/2	23.758	17.27	23	415.47	72.25	56	2463.0	175.9	91	6503.8	285.8
6	28.274	18.84	1/2	433.73	73.82	57	2551.7	179.0	92	6647.6	289.0
1/2	33.183	20.42	24	452.39	75.39	58	2642.0	182.2	93	6792.9	292.1
7	38.484	21.99	1/2	471.43	76.96	59	2733.9	185.3	94	6939.7	295.3
1/2	44.178	23.56	25	490.87	78.54	60	2827.4	188.4	95	7088.2	298.4
8	50.265	25.13	26	530.93	81.68	61	2922.4	191.6	96	7238.2	301.5
1/2	56.745	26.70	27	572.55	84.82	62	3019.0	194.7	97	7389.8	304.7
9	63.617	28.27	28	615.75	87.96	63	3117.2	197.9	98	7542.9	307.8
1/2	70.882	29.84	29	660.52	91.10	64	3216.9	201.0	99	7697.7	311.0

Weight Calculation

Weight of round iron per foot = Diameter (quarter inches) squared × 0.1666
Weight of flat iron per foot = Width × thickness × 3.333
Weight of plates per sq. ft. = 5 pounds for each $\frac{1}{8}$ inch in thickness
Weight of chain = Diameter squared × 10.7 (approximate)
Safe load (pounds) for chain = Bar diameter (quarter inches) squared × 2000

To compute weight of metal from weight of pattern, with no allowance for cores or runners, multiply as follows:

Multiplication Factors

White Pine	Mahogany	Result
16.7	10.7	Cast iron
18	12.2	Brass
23	15.	Lead
15	9.	Tin
16	10.4	Zinc

Weight of brass pattern × .9 = weight of iron casting, approximately.

Specific Gravities and Weights of Metals

Material	Specific Gravity	Weight per Cubic Inch (pounds)
Water, at 39.1° F.	1.	.036
Aluminum	2.6	.094
Antimony, cast 6.64 to 6.74	6.7	.237
Bismuth	9.74	.352
Brass, cast 7.8 to 8.4	8.1	.30
Bronze 8.4 to 8.6	8.5	.305
Copper, cast 8.6 to 8.8	8.7	.32
Gold, pure, 24 carat	19.25	.70
Iron, cast 6.9 to 7.4	7.21	.263
Iron, wrought 7.6 to 7.9	7.77	.281
Lead	11.4	.41
Mercury, at 60° F.	13.58	.49
Platinum 21. to 22.	21.5	.775
Silver	10.5	.386
Steel, average	7.8	.283
Spelter or zinc 6.8 to 7.2	7.	.26
Tin, cast 7.2 to 7.5	7.35	.262

Pressure In Molds

Depth (ft.) (in.)	Pounds (per sq. in.)	Depth (ft.) (in.)	Pounds (per sq. in.)	Depth (ft.) (in.)	Pounds (per sq. in.)
1	.26	19	4.94	3 6	10.92
2	.52	20	5.20	4	12.48
3	.78	21	5.46	4 6	14.04
4	1.04	22	5.72	5	15.60
5	1.30	23	5.98	5 6	17.16
6	1.56	2 00	6.24	6	18.72
7	1.82	25	6.50	6 6	20.28
8	2.08	26	6.76	7	21.84
9	2.34	27	7.02	7 6	23.40
10	2.60	28	7.28	8	24.96
11	2.86	29	7.54	8 6	26.52
1 00	3.12	2 6	7.80	9	28.08
13	3.38	31	8.06	9 6	29.64
14	3.64	32	8.32	10	31.20
15	3.90	33	8.58	10 6	32.76
16	4.16	34	8.84	11	34.32
17	4.42	35	9.10	11 6	35.88
1 6	4.68	3 00	9.36	12	37.44

To find the total lifting pressure on the cope, multiply the pressure per square inch at a given depth below the pouring basin by the area (square inches) of the surface acted against. The result is in pounds.

Temperatures*

Connection	Heat (Degrees Fahrenheit)
Core ovens	250 to 450
Bright iron becomes yellow	435
Bright iron becomes purple	500
Bright iron becomes indigo	550
Bright iron becomes gray	750
Tin melts	445
Mercury boils	660
Lead melts	612
Zinc melts	775
Silver melts	1775
Copper melts	1885
Gold melts	1900
Iron bar red in a dark room, just visible	950
Iron bar red in ordinary office	1075
Iron bar red in daylight, open air	1450
Cast iron melts white	2075
Cast iron melts gray	2230
Steel melts	2750
Annealing malleable iron	1600 to 1750

*From late scientific investigations

INDEX

INDEX

A

	PAGE
Air furnace for melting malleable iron	154
Alloys, brass and bronze	167
Analysis of cast iron	190
arbitration bar	191
Keep's mechanical	190
Analysis of cupola mixtures, chemical	123
Annealing malleable-iron castings	161
oven for	165
Annealing steel castings	144
Arbitration-bar tests of cast iron	191
specifications for	191
test bar in	191
Arbors for core work	56, 63

B

Balanced cores	60
Barrel cores, making	92
Batch sand mixer	152
Binders, core	9, 47, 51
Blast	112
fan-blower	112
gage for	114
pressure-blower	113
Blowholes	22, 31
Bottom doors, cupola-furnace	109
Brass	167
chip separation	182
cleaning castings of	181
heats, size of	174
melting	176
molding equipment	172
molding materials	171
molding process	174
pattern weight	194
specific gravity and weight	195
work, examples of	175
Brass work	167
alloys in	167
production processes in	171
Breast, cupola-furnace	111
Bronze	168
specific gravity and weight of	195

C

	PAGE
Carbon	121, 136
Cast-iron analysis	190
Casting operations	109
brass work	167
malleable practice	145
melting gray iron	109
steel work	136
Centrifugal sand mixer	129
Chaplets	21
setting	60
Charcoal foundry facing	7
Charging door, cupola-furnace	112
Cheek	9
Clamps	17
Clay wash	8
Cleaning castings, methods of	131
malleable-iron work, in	160
steel work, in	144
Coke, foundry	126
Cold-shuts	31
Cope	9
flat joint, for	33
floor bedding, in	44
loam molding, in	99, 102, 105
pressure head on	28
Coping out	35
Copper	168
specific gravity and weight	195
temperature, melting	196
Core-making machines	57
Core ovens	48
Core plates	48
racks for	50
Core sand	6, 46
mixtures	51
Core work	2, 46
barrel	92
for brass molding	175
dry-sand	46
general equipment for	48
green-sand	39, 62
for malleable-iron molding	152
setting cores in	58
for steel molding	141
Core-rod straightening machine	134
Cover core	90
Cover plates in loam molding	95, 105
Crucible malleable-iron melting	152

INDEX

	PAGE
Cupola furnace	109
mixtures for	120
operation of	116
parts of	109
Cupola malleable-iron melting	153
Cutting and tempering sand	19

D

Drag	9
flat-joint	32
floor-bedding pit	43
Draw sticks	17
Drawback	100
Drying stove for brass molds	173
Dry-sand cores	46
equipment for making	48
methods of making	53
materials for	46
setting of	58
use of	51
Dry-sand molding	2, 89
Duplicating of castings, multiple	66
brass	176
gated-pattern method	67
jolt ramming machine	79
machine molding	67
malleable-iron	148
permanent match	67
roller ramming machine	86
roll-over machine	73, 77
squeezer machine	71, 75, 86
stripping-plate machine	68

F

Facings	6
dry-sand core	47, 51
for steel molding	137
Ferrosilicon in malleable iron	158
Fire clay	7
Fire sand	5
Flasks for	9
brass molding	172
malleable-iron molding	152
steel molding	138
Flat joint	32
Floor bedding	23, 42
Foremen, duties of	188
Foundry, typical	182
cleaning department	187

Foundry, typical (continued)
- core shop 185
- cranes 187
- cupolas 184
- floor plan 183
- heavy-molding division 185
- light-molding division 185
- molding machines 186
- pattern room 184
- shop office 184
- storage of materials 186
- tracks 186
- type of building 183
- unloading of materials 186
- ventilation 183

Foundry work 1–196
- casting operations 109
- molding practice 1
- practical data 192
- shop management 182

Free sands 6

G

Gaggers 21
Gas furnace for brass melting 179
Gated patterns for duplicate castings 67
Gating 24
Graphite foundry facing 7
Gray iron 109
Green-sand cores 39, 62
Green-sand molding 1
- principles of 18
- typical problems in 31

H

Hard-rolling of castings 160
Heat, running a 116
- for brass work 174
- for malleable casting 159
- for steel casting 141

I

Iron 109
- specific gravity and weight of 195
- temperature indications 196

J

Jointing 32
- loam molds 100

INDEX

K

Keep's mechanical analysis of cast iron	190
chilled depth	190
deductions by	191
silicon and shrinkage	190
transverse strength	190

L

Labor, shop management of foundry	188
foremen	188
laborers	188
molders	188
superintendent	188
Laborers, duties of foundry	188
Ladles for	118
brass work	177
malleable-iron work	159
steel work	142
Laying up loam mold	99
Lead	169
melting temperature	196
specific gravity and weight of	195
Lifters	15
Lifting ring, core	40
Lining	111
cupola-furnace	111
foundry-ladle	118
Loam mixtures	92
Loam molding	2, 94
example of complex cylinder	104
example of simple	102
materials for	97
principles of	99
rigging for	94

M

Malleable cast iron	145
annealing	161, 196
cleaning	160
finishing	167
melting, methods of	152
metal characteristics	145
method of casting	159
methods of testing	146
mixture for	156
molding	148
patterns for	148
specifications for	146

	PAGE
Malleable practice	145
development of	145
production processes	148
Manganese	122, 136
Match, sand	36
permanent oil	67
Materials, molding	3
brick for loam molding	97
cinders	98
facings	6, 98
miscellaneous	7
mud for loam molding	98
sands	3, 171
Melting	109
brass	176
malleable-iron	152
principles of iron	115
steel	141
supplementary operations in iron	127
Mixing machines, sand	128
Mixing of sand	127
Mixtures, cupola-furnace	120
calculation of	124
chemical analysis of	123
elements in	121
fuel in	126
proportions of charge in	126
Mold board	9
Molders, duties of	188
Molding machines	67
Molding practice	1
brass	167
divisions of iron molding	1
general molding equipment	3
malleable-iron	145
processes	18
steel	137, 143

N

Natural-draft furnace for brass work	177
Nowel or drag	9

O

Open sand molding	45
Open-hearth malleable-iron melting	156
Open-hearth steel, casting	141

P

Packing steel molds	139
Parting dusts	8

INDEX

	PAGE
Patterns for malleable castings	148
Phosphor bronze	171
phosphor tin in	171
Phosphorus	122, 136, 170
Pickling castings	133
of brass and bronze	181
Pig iron in malleable work	157
Pouring	119
brass	174
loam molds	104, 106
malleable iron	159
short	31
steel	142
venting action during	23
Practical data	192
circular areas and circumferences	194
conversion factors	193
mensuration	193
percentage, examples of using	192
pressure in molds	195
specific gravities and weights	195
square box measure	193
temperatures	196
weight of metal and patterns	194
weights, molding material	193
Pressure in molds	27, 195
pressure distribution examples	28
pressure-head examples	28
Pyrometer for annealing furnace	167

R

Ramming	20
Ramming machine	79
jar or jolt	79
roller	86
Rammers	13
core work, for	48
Rapping plate	17
Rattler or tumbling barrel	131
Reinforcement, core	47, 55
Risers	22
Roll-over machine	73
power type	77
Rotary sieve	129
Runners	24

S

Safety-first factors	189
clothing	189
personal	189

INDEX

Safety-first factors (continued)
    shop equipment ... 189
Sand shaker ... 129
Sand-blasting ... 135
Sands, molding ... 3
    core sand ... 6, 46
    elements in ... 4
    fire sand ... 5
    for brass work ... 171
    for malleable iron work ... 149
    for steel work ... 137
    free sands ... 6
    grades of ... 5
    green-sand mixture ... 18
    volume per ton ... 193
Scabs ... 31
Scrap iron in malleable work ... 157
Sea-coal foundry facing ... 7
Setting cores ... 58
Shop management ... 182
    governing factors in ... 182
    labor ... 188
    of typical foundry ... 182
    physical results ... 190
    safety first in ... 189
Shovel ... 12
Shrinkage cracks ... 31
Shrinkage heads or feeders ... 26
Shrinkage in malleable casting ... 148
Shrinkage in steel work ... 137
Sieve, riddle or foundry ... 13, 129
Sifting ... 19
Silicon ... 122, 136
Skimming gate ... 24
Slag hole, cupola-furnace ... 111
Slicks ... 15
    corner ... 16
Slip or skinning loam ... 94
Snap flask ... 9
Spill trough for brass pouring ... 173
Spindle for loam mold sweeping ... 94
Split-pattern molds ... 38
    core lifting ring ... 40
    green-sand core ... 39
    loose-piece ... 39
    three-part ... 41
Spraying can for core work ... 48
Sprues ... 24
Squeezer machine ... 71

INDEX

Squeezer machine (continued)
    automatic 86
    power type 75
Steel 137
    annealing castings of 144
    casting, running a heat for 141
    cleaning castings of 144
    cores in molding 141
    facings for, mold 137
    flasks for molding 138
    molds for, setting up 143
    packing process in molding 139
    specific gravity and weight of 195
    temperature, melting 196
Steel work 136
    casting 141
    molding 137
Stripping-plate machine 68
Sulphur 122, 136
Superintendent, duties of 188
Swabs 16
Sweeping 95
    cores 56
Swells 31

T

Tables
    alloys, proportions of mixtures in 170
    arbitration-bar standards for cast iron 192
    crucible sizes 176
    cupola-furnace sizes 112
    fan-blower performance 113
    flasks, sizes of wooden 11
    ladle data, foundry- 118
    phosphor-bronze mixtures 171
    sands, proportions of elements in 4
Tapping 117
Tempering 19
    cores, dry-sand 47
Testing cast iron 191
    malleable 146
Three-part mold 41
Tin 168
    specific gravity and weight of 195
    temperature, melting 196
Tools, hand-molding 9
    for finishing 14
    for brass work 172
Trowels 15, 48

	PAGE
Tumbling castings	131
Tuyères	111

V

Vent rods	16
Ventilation systems in typical foundry	183
Venting	22
dry-sand cores	47
loam molds	100, 106

W

Warping	31
White iron in malleable practice	149

Z

Zinc	169
melting temperature	196

CPSIA information can be obtained at www.ICGtesting.com
Printed in the USA
LVOW03s2248191014

409511LV00006B/18/P